CROCKERY
COOKING

BY ALEXIS DURRELL

WEATHERVANE BOOKS
NEW YORK

A COLANDER AND A LARGE SAUCEPAN, OR SERVING BOWL,
CREATE THE EASIEST METHOD OF EMPTYING LIQUID FROM
YOUR CROCKERY-POT.

IF THE LIQUID SEEMS UNUSUALLY GREASY (AS WHEN YOU
COOK OXTAILS):   REFRIGERATE, OR PUT ICECUBES IN
THE LIQUID - THIS WILL CAUSE THE FAT TO RISE SO
IT MAY BE REMOVED BEFORE USING THE LIQUID FOR
COOKING PASTA, VEGETABLES, OR SOUP.

INTRODUCTION

THE 191 RECIPES ARE ARRANGED ALPHABETICALLY BY THE
PRINCIPAL INGREDIENT (BEEF / SHORT RIBS), OR BY THE
TYPE OF FOOD (PUDDING / CHOCOLATE) - AN INDEX ON
PAGES 79 AND 80 CROSS-REFERENCES ALL RECIPES.

CHICKEN DOES NOT REQUIRE ALL-DAY COOKING; SO MAY
BE STARTED BY THE USE OF AN ELECTRIC TIMER AT NOON,
FOR AN EVENING MEAL.

FISH DOES NOT REQUIRE EXTENDED COOKING; SO IS NOT WELL
SUITED TO CROCKERY-POT METHODS, EXCEPT AS A LATE
ADDITION TO A "SAUCE" OR "CREAM" RECIPE. SHELLFISH,
HAVING THE FIRMEST TEXTURE, ARE THE MOST ADAPTABLE
TO CROCKERY-POT COOKING.

RICE CAN BE COOKED IN THE CROCKERY-POT, SET AT "HIGH";
BUT IT MUST BE STIRRED FREQUENTLY. IF COOKED FOR
EXTENDED PERIODS AT "LOW", THE OUTER SHELL OF THE
RICE GRAIN WILL SPLIT AND THE STARCHY INTERIOR WILL
FORM A VERY GUMMY RICE-PASTE.

APPLES/BAKED

6-8 BAKING APPLES, CORED CAREFULLY
                   SO NOT CUT THROUGH
                   THE BOTTOM (OR ALL
                   THE FILLING WILL
                   DRAIN-OUT DURING
                   COOKING)

                                              PLACE IN
                                              CROCKERY-POT

                                              COOK AT LOW,
RAISINS, MUSCAT OR SEEDLESS   ALL DAY, OR
BROWN SUGAR   OVERNIGHT
HONEY   MIX TO A THICK
1-2 T CINNAMON   PASTE, STUFF   SERVE WARM
1 TSP NUTMEG   CORED APPLES   OR COLD WITH
BUTTER OR MARGARINE   CREAM OR
                                              CONDENSED
                                              MILK

APPLESAUCE

8-10 APPLES, PEELED, CORED, SLICED
            OR: JUST CORED & QUARTERED
                                              PLACE IN
1/2 C   WATER   CROCKERY-POT
1/2 C   GRANULATED SUGAR
1/2 C   BROWN SUGAR   COOK AT LOW,
2 T   CINNAMON   ALL DAY
1 TSP   NUTMEG
1/2 TSP CLOVES, GROUND
1 T   BUTTER
1-3 T   LEMON JUICE

ARTICHOKES

ARTICHOKES, SHARP TIPS REMOVED   PLACE IN CROCKERY-POT
SALT
2 T   LEMON JUICE OR VINEGAR   COOK AT LOW, ALL DAY
2 C   BOULLION OR WATER
                                   SERVE HOT WITH MELTED
                                   BUTTER OR MAYONNAISE

                                   SERVE COLD WITH SAUCE
                                   MADE OF MAYONNAISE
                                   LIGHTLY SEASONED WITH
                                   MUSTARD, ONION SALT

5

BARBECUE MEATS

MEAT TO FILL CROCKERY-POT, TRIMMED OF AS MUCH
    FAT AS POSSIBLE. IF USING SPARE-RIBS,
    BROIL FOR 20 OR 30 MINUTES TO MELT-OFF
    HIDDEN FAT

GARLIC SALT
PEPPER
2 ONIONS, CHOPPED
1 (14-16 OUNCE) BOTTLE OF BARBECUE SAUCE
1/4 TSP LIQUID SMOKE (OPTIONAL)

PLACE IN
CROCKERY-POT

COOK AT LOW,
ALL DAY

BEANS/BAR-B-Q

1 POUND DRIED NAVY BEANS, SOAKED OVERNIGHT
    IN SEVERAL QUARTS OF WATER, THEN
    CLEANED AND DRAINED

1 LB BACON, DICED,   THEN FRIED TO REMOVE FAT
4 C   TOMATO JUICE
2   ONIONS, CHOPPED

1 CAN   TOMATO SAUCE
1/2 C   BROWN SUGAR, FIRMLY PACKED
1 TSP   GARLIC SALT
1 T   WORCESTERSHIRE SAUCE
1 T   SOY SAUCE

OR, USE
1 (16 OUNCE)
BOTTLE OF
BARBECUE
SAUCE

PLACE
IN
CROCKERY-
POT

COOK
AT LOW,
ALL DAY

6

BEANS/BOSTON

1 POUND DRIED NAVY BEANS, GREAT NORTHERN
    BEANS, MARROWFAT BEANS, OR PEA
    BEANS; SOAKED OVERNIGHT IN
    SEVERAL QUARTS OF WATER, THEN
    CLEANED AND DRAINED

1/4 LB SALT PORK, OR PICKLED PORK, CUBED
6 C   WATER
1-2   ONIONS, CHOPPED
1/3 C BROWN SUGAR, FIRMLY PACKED
1/4 C DARK MOLASSES
1   C CATSUP
1-2 TSP DRY MUSTARD
1 T   SALT

PLACE IN
CROCKERY-POT

COOK AT LOW,
ALL DAY

BEANS/CHILI

1/2 POUND DRIED PINTO, PINK, OR KIDNEY
    BEANS; SOAKED OVERNIGHT, DRAINED.
    OR, USE 2 LARGE CANS OF KIDNEY
    BEANS, DRAINED

2 POUNDS STEW MEAT, DICED; OR CHUCK
    STEAK, COARSELY GROUND. BROWN
    IN SKILLET AND DRAIN
2 (16 OUNCE) CANS STEWED TOMATOES
1 CAN TOMATO PASTE
2 C WATER, IF USING DRIED BEANS WHICH
        HAVE BEEN SOAKED

1 BELL PEPPER, CHOPPED
1-2 ONIONS, CHOPPED
2-3 T CHILI POWDER
2 CLOVES GARLIC, MINCED OR CRUSHED
1/2 TSP CUMIN OR TABASCO

PLACE IN
CROCKERY-POT

COOK AT LOW,
ALL DAY

BEANS/COMBINATION

1 LB GROUND BEEF, BROWNED AND DRAINED
1 LB BACON, DICED, BROWNED AND DRAINED
3 LARGE ONIONS, IN THICK SLICES
1 LARGE CAN PORK AND BEANS
1 LARGE CAN KIDNEY BEANS, DRAINED
1 LARGE CAN LIMA BEANS, DRAINED
1 (16 OUNCE) CAN STEWED TOMATOES
1/2 C BROWN SUGAR, FIRMLY PACKED
1/4 C VINEGAR
1 TSP SALT
PEPPER

PLACE IN
CROCKERY-POT

COOK AT LOW,
ALL DAY

7

BEANS/MEXICAN

```
1 POUND DRIED KIDNEY BEANS, WASHED     PUT INTO
         AND DRAINED                   LARGE PAN,
3 C   WATER                            BRING TO A
2 C   RED WINE                         BOIL, REMOVE
                                       FROM STOVE;    PLACE
                                       LET SOAK       IN
                                       OVERNIGHT,     CROCKERY-
                                       DO NOT DRAIN   POT

OR, USE 4 CANS KIDNEY BEANS                           COOK
                                                      AT LOW,
1 OR 2 ONIONS, IN CHUNKS                              ALL DAY
1 CAN   STEWED TOMATOES
2 CLOVES  GARLIC, MINCED OR CRUSHED
1 T   SALT
1 T   DRY MUSTARD
2-3 T   CHILI POWDER
1/4 C   VINEGAR

2 T SUGAR
1 STICK CINNAMON
1/4 TSP CLOVES
```

BEANS/PINEAPPLE

```
1 POUND DRIED PEA BEANS, OR PINK BEANS;
        SOAKED OVERNIGHT IN SEVERAL
        QUARTS OF WATER, THEN CLEANED      PLACE IN
        AND DRAINED                        CROCKERY-POT
3/4 LB  BACON, DICED,  BROWNED AND DRAINED
1-2  ONIONS, CHOPPED                        COOK AT LOW,
1 TSP   DRY MUSTARD                         ALL DAY
1/2 TSP SALT
1/4 C   HOT CHILI SAUCE
1 CAN   CRUSHED PINEAPPLE, INCLUDING LIQUID
```

BEANS/PINK

```
1 POUND DRIED PINK BEANS, SOAKED OVERNIGHT
         AND DRAINED
HAMBONE WITH HAM, OR HAM HOCKS               PLACE IN
2 LARGE ONIONS, CHOPPED                      CROCKERY-POT
2-3 TSP   GARLIC SALT
2 CANS    TOMATO SAUCE                        COOK AT LOW,
3 C       TOMATO JUICE OR WATER               ALL DAY
```

8

```
3-5 POUND POT ROAST, TO FIT POT    DREDGE IN       PLACE IN
1/4 C OIL                          FLOUR, AND      CROCKERY-POT
FLOUR                              BROWN IN
                                   OIL             COOK AT LOW,
                                                   ALL DAY
4-5 ONIONS, SLICED THICK
2 CLOVES  GARLIC, MINCED
1 CAN   BEER
1 T     VINEGAR
1/2     BAY LEAF, CRUSHED
1 T     SALT
```

```
4 POTATOES, PEELED & CUBED
4 CARROTS, SCRAPED & CHUNKED
1 STALK CELERY, CUBED                PLACE IN CROCKERY-POT
2 ONIONS, CHOPPED                    IN ORDER LISTED
                                     (VEGETABLES ON BOTTOM)
3-4 POT ROAST OR BRISKET
1 CAN BOULLION                       COOK AT LOW, ALL DAY
1 CUP WATER
1/2 C RED WINE

2 T PARSLEY
2 TSP SALT
1/4 TSP PEPPER
1 T WORCESTERSHIRE SAUCE
1 BAY LEAF, ON TOP, SO IT WILL
           EASY TO REMOVE
```

9

BEEF/BURGUNDY

6 SLICES BACON, DICED, FRIED IN LARGE SKILLET;
        REMOVE BACON, PUT INTO CROCKERY-POT

		PLACE IN CROCKERY-POT
2-3 LBS STEW MEAT, CUBED FLOUR BACON GREASE	DREDGE IN FLOUR, BROWN IN BACON GREASE	COOK AT LOW, ALL DAY

2 ONIONS, SLICED
1 CARROT, SLICED THINLY
1 LARGE TOMATO, SLICED

1 1/2 TSP SALT
1/4 TSP PEPPER
1 TSP PAPRIKA
3 CLOVES GARLIC, MINCED
1/2 TSP THYME
1 T TOMATO PASTE

3 C BURGUNDY WINE
1 CAN BEEF BROTH (BOULLION)

1 BAY LEAF, ON TOP, FOR EASY EASY REMOVAL

1/2 - 1 LB FRESH MUSHROOMS, SLICED BUTTER	SAUTE, STIR INTO CROCKERY-POT JUST BEFORE SERVING

BEEF/CHILI

2-3 LBS FLANK STEAK, CUT IN
    PIECES, POUNDED WITH
    THE EDGE OF A SAUCER
    TO TENDERIZE; OR SHORT
    RIBS WITH FAT REMOVED
1 C FLOUR
2 TSP SALT
2 T CHILI POWDER
OIL
	DREDGE IN
	FLOUR AND
	SEASONINGS,
	BROWN IN
	OIL
		PLACE IN CROCKERY-POT
		
		COOK AT LOW, ALL DAY

2 CLOVES GARLIC, MINCED
2 ONIONS, CHOPPED
2 BELL PEPPERS, CHOPPED
4 C TOMATOES, CHOPPED
    OR 2 CANS WHOLE
    TOMATOES, DRAINED
1/2 C HOT CHILI SAUCE
1 TSP GARLIC SALT

3 CARROTS, SCRAPED AND CUT IN CHUNKS,
    PUT IN BOTTOM OF CROCKERY-POT
3 LB CORNED BEEF BRISKET
2-3 ONIONS, QUARTERED
2-3 CELERY TOPS
1 CLOVE GARLIC, MINCED
1-2 TURNIPS, IN CHUNKS
2-3 POTATOES, IN CHUNKS TO FILL
    CROCKERY-POT 1-INCH FROM TOP
1- 1 1/2 C WATER, DO NOT FILL CROCKERY-
        POT TO THE TOP, IT WILL
        OVERFLOW DURING COOKING.
        FILL ONLY TO 1/2-INCH
        FROM TOP

PLACE IN
CROCKERY-POT IN
ORDER LISTED

COOK AT LOW,
ALL DAY

DRAIN CROCKERY-POT
THROUGH COLANDER
INTO A LARGE
SAUCEPAN, LEAVING
MEAT & VEGETABLES
IN CROCKERY-POT

LIQUID FROM CROCKERY-POT
ADDITIONAL WATER, IF NECESSARY
1 CABBAGE, CUT INTO 8 PIECES

IN LARGE SAUCEPAN,
COOK CABBAGE IN BOILING
LIQUID, BEING SURE NOT
TO OVERCOOK; SERVE WITH
CORNED BEEF & VEGETABLES

BEEF/EGGPLANT, ZUCCHINI

2 LBS BEEF, CUBED
OIL

BROWN
IN OIL

PLACE IN CROCKERY-POT

COOK AT LOW, ALL DAY

3 ONIONS, SLICED
3 TOMATOES, SLICED
1 BELL PEPPER, SLICED INTO RINGS
2 TSP SALT
PEPPER

1/2 - 1 C LIQUID FROM CROCKERY-POT
        (ADD WATER, IF NECESSARY)
3 STALKS CELERY, SLICED
2 C EGGPLANT, CUBED
3 ZUCCHINI, SLICED
1 TOMATO, SLICED

IN SAUCEPAN WITH LID,
STEAM QUICKLY IN
BOILING LIQUID,
DO NOT OVERCOOK;
MIX WITH MEAT BEFORE
SERVING

BEEF/FLANK STEAK, STUFFED

1 LARGE   FLANK STEAK, POUNDED
          THIN-AS-POSSIBLE WITH
          EDGE OF SAUCER OR
          MEAT MALLET

1 (6-1/2 OUNCE) PACKAGE
          DRY CORNBREAD STUFFING
          MIX
1/3 C BACON GREASE, OR 1 CUBE
                      MARGARINE
3/4 C BEEF BROTH (BOULLION)
1-2   EGGS
3-4   STALKS CELERY, CHOPPED
1-2   ONIONS, CHOPPED
3T   DRIED PARSLEY
SEASONED SALT, TO TASTE
PEPPER

MIX
STUFFING

PUT ON
FLANK
STEAK
1 TO 1 1/2
INCH THICK

ROLL-UP,
AS YOU
WOULD A
JELLY-ROLL;
TIE WITH
COTTON TWINE

PLACE ROLLED
AND TIED
MEAT IN
CROCKERY-POT

PUT ANY
EXTRA
STUFFING IN
FOIL AND
SEAL TIGHTLY,
PLACE ON TOP
OF MEAT IN
CROCKERY-POT

COOK AT LOW,
ALL DAY

BEEF/FRUIT

3-4 LB   POT ROAST; CUT IN HALF, IF
         NECESSARY, TO FIT CROCKERY-POT
1 TSP   SALT
PEPPER
12-15 DRIED APRICOTS
12-15 DRIED PRUNES, PITTED
1 SMALL ONION, CHOPPED
1 T   CINNAMON
1/2 TSP   GINGER
1/2 C   RAISINS, MUSCAT OR SEEDLESS
1/2 C   PORT WINE

PLACE MEAT AND
"DRY" INGREDIENTS
ON LARGE, WIDE PIECE
OF FOIL; SEAL TOP AND
ONE SIDE TIGHTLY

POUR SWEET WINE INTO
POUCH BEFORE SEALING
LAST SIDE

PLACE IN CROCKERY-POT;
COOK AT LOW, ALL DAY

BEEF/GOULASH

2 LBS BEEF, IN CHUNKS ‖ DREDGE IN FLOUR,
FLOUR   ‖ BROWN IN OIL
OIL

                                PLACE IN
                                CROCKERY-POT

1 CLOVE GARLIC, MINCED
3-4 ONIONS, SLICED   COOK AT LOW,
1 1/2 TSP CARAWAY SEED   ALL DAY
1/2 TSP MARJORAM
1/4 TSP THYME   PRIOR TO
1 1/2 T PAPRIKA   SERVING, TURN-OFF
1 TSP SALT   AND ALLOW TO COOL
1/2 TSP PEPPER
1 T VINEGAR
1/2 C RED WINE, BURGUNDY

1/2 - 1 C SOUR CREAM ‖ ADD TO COOLED GOULASH IN
                            CROCKERY-POT (SOUR CREAM WILL
                            CURDLE & SEPARATE IF ADDED TO
                            HOT LIQUID)

                            SERVE WITH
                            BUTTERED NOODLES

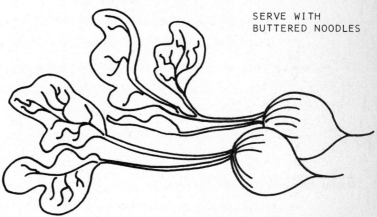

BEEF/GREEN BEANS

2-3 LBS BEEF, IN CHUNKS
1 TSP GARLIC SALT
1 TSP GARLIC JUICE
PEPPER   PLACE IN CROCKERY-POT
1 T PAPRIKA
2 T SOY SAUCE   COOK AT LOW, ALL DAY
1 T WORCESTERSHIRE SAUCE
1 CAN STEWED TOMATOES
1 16-OUNCE BAG FROZEN FRENCH CUT
               GREEN BEANS
1 ONION, SLICED INTO THIN RINGS

13

BEEF/HAMBURGER CASSEROLE

2 LBS HAMBURGER, BROWNED & DRAINED
2-3 POTATOES, SLICED, <u>OR</u> 1 C RICE
3 CARROTS, SLICED
2 ONIONS, CHOPPED
3 STALKS CELERY, SLICED
2 CANS STEWED TOMATOES

1 T   CHILI POWDER
2 CLOVES   GARLIC, MINCED
1 1/2 TSP   SALT
PEPPER
SOY SAUCE
WORCESTERSHIRE SAUCE
DRIED PARSLEY FLAKES

PLACE IN CROCKERY-POT

COOK AT LOW, ALL DAY

BEEF/HAMBURGER, SLOPPY JOES

3 LBS HAMBURGER, BROWNED & DRAINED
    OR, STEW MEAT, CHOPPED
2-3 ONIONS, CHOPPED
1 BELL PEPPER, CHOPPED
2 TOMATOES, CHOPPED

GARLIC JUICE, TO TASTE
SALT
PEPPER

2 (6-OUNCE) CANS TOMATO PASTE

PLACE IN CROCKERY-POT

COOK AT LOW, ALL DAY

SERVE ON WARM ONION
ROLLS, OR HAMBURGER
BUNS. GARNISH WITH
CHOPPED GREEN ONION
TOPS AND/OR GRATED
CHEDDAR CHEESE

BEEF/HEART, CURRIED

1-2 LBS HEART, SLICED THIN
1 T   CURRY POWDER
1 TSP   TUMERIC
1/2 TSP   CHILI POWDER
1/8 TSP   CAYENNE

PLACE IN CROCKERY-POT

COOK AT LOW, ALL DAY

2 T   CORNSTARCH OR FLOUR
1/3 C   COLD WATER

MIX TOGETHER, TO DISSOLVE WITHOUT
LUMPS; ADD TO CROCKERY-POT TO
THICKEN LIQUID

3-4 SLICES BACON, DICED, BROWNED & DRAINED
2 T   BACON GREASE, OR MARGARINE
1 1/2 C   WATER, BOILING
1 C   QUICK-COOKING BROWN RICE

SERVE CURRIED HEART
STRIPS OVER BROWN
RICE; WITH RAISINS,
CHOPPED BOILED EGGS,
MINCED ONIONS, NUTS,
CHOPPED GREEN ONION
TOPS, CHUTNEY

14

BEEF/HEART, FRUIT

1 WHOLE BEEF HEART, CLEANED OF ALL MEMBRANES AND FAT. SCORED LIGHTLY INSIDE & OUT, AND SPRINKLED WITH A SMALL AMOUNT OF MEAT TENDERIZER		PLACE IN CROCKERY-POT
12-14 DRIED APRICOTS		ADD WINE
12-14 DRIED PRUNES, PITTED		
1/2 C RAISINS, MUSCAT OR SEEDLESS	STUFF	COOK AT LOW,
1 APPLE, PEELED AND CHOPPED	HEART	ALL DAY
1/4 TSP NUTMEG		
1/4 TSP CINNAMON		
1-2 ONIONS, CHOPPED FINELY		
3/4 C PORT WINE		

BEEF/HEART, PAPRIKA

3 LBS SLICED BEEF HEART, CLEANED OF ALL MEMBRANES AND FAT. SLICED INTO 1/4-INCH STRIPS	PLACE IN CROCKERY-POT
2 ENVELOPES GOULASH SEASONING MIX	COOK AT LOW,
2 ONIONS, SLICED	ALL DAY
2 (16-OUNCE) CANS STEWED TOMATOES	
	SERVE OVER BUTTERED WIDE NOODLES

BEEF/HEART, STUFFED

1 WHOLE BEEF HEART, CLEANED OF ALL MEMBRANES AND FAT. SCORED LIGHTLY INSIDE & OUT, AND SPRINKLED WITH A SMALL AMOUNT OF TENDERIZER		STUFF HEART
1/2 C WATER, BOILING	ADD TO STUFFING	PLACE IN CROCKERY-POT
1 CUBE MARGARINE	INGREDIENTS BELOW	
2 BEEF BOULLION CUBES		ADD BOULLION
1 (6 1/2-OUNCE) PKG CORNMEAL DRESSING MIX		COOK AT LOW,
1 ONION, MINCED		ALL DAY
3/4 C CELERY, CHOPPED		
1 EGG		
1 ENVELOPE ITALIAN SALAD DRESSING MIX		
1 CAN BOULLION (BEEF BROTH)		

15

BEEF/HEART, SWEET & SOUR

3 LBS SLICED BEEF HEART, CLEANED OF ALL
      MEMBRANES AND FAT. SLICED INTO   PLACE IN
      1/4-INCH STRIPS   CROCKERY-POT
1 CAN   PINEAPPLE CHUNKS & SYRUP
1/4 C   CORNSTARCH DISSOLVED IN A LITTLE   COOK AT LOW,
          COLD WATER, TO AVOID LUMPS   ALL DAY
1 ONION, THINLY SLICED
2 TOMATOES, CHOPPED   SERVE OVER
1/2 C   VINEGAR   STEAMED WHITE
3 WHOLE CLOVES   RICE, GARNISHED
1/8 TSP ALLSPICE   WITH SESAME
1/2 C   BROWN SUGAR   SEEDS
2 T   SOY SAUCE

BEEF/HORSERADISH

1   3-4 LB. POT ROAST, WITH ALL FAT REMOVED
    (FLAVOR WILL BE BETTER, IF BEEF IS   PLACE IN
    BROWNED IN OIL BEFORE PUTTING INTO   CROCKERY-POT
    CROCKERY-POT)
2 TSP SALT   COOK AT LOW,
1/2 TSP PEPPER   ALL DAY
1 ONION, CHOPPED
1 CAN TOMATO PASTE
1/3 C HORSERADISH

BEEF/KIDNEY STEW

1 POUND   STEAK, CUBED
1 KIDNEY, CLEANED, CUBED*   DREDGE IN FLOUR,
FLOUR   BROWN IN OIL   PLACE IN
OIL   CROCKERY-POT

3/4 C   RED WINE, BURGUNDY   COOK AT LOW,
2 TSP   SALT   ALL DAY
1/8 TSP OREGANO
1/8 TSP ROSEMARY
1/8 TSP THYME
1/8 TSP BASIL
2 T   DRIED PARSLEY
1   ONION, CHOPPED

1 POUND MUSHROOMS, SLICED   SAUTE, ADD TO CROCKERY-POT
BUTTER   JUST BEFORE SERVING

    *NOTE: KIDNEY HAS A VERY STRONG "LIVER" FLAVOR

BEEF/MUSHROOMS

```
2-3 LBS  BEEF, CUBED
1 ENVELOPE BEEF-MUSHROOM SOUP MIX        PUT IN CROCKERY-POT
1/3 C  BURGUNDY WINE
SEASONED SALT                            COOK AT LOW, ALL DAY
PEPPER
1/2 ONION, MINCED                        DRAIN (KEEP LIQUID FOR
                                         FUTURE USE)


1-2 LB   MUSHROOMS, SLICED        SAUTE, ADD TO DRAINED MEAT IN
BUTTER                            CROCKERY-POT; SERVE OVER NOODLES
```

BEEF/ONIONS

```
2-3 LBS  BEEF, CUBED
1 ENVELOPE ONION SOUP MIX              PUT IN CROCKERY-POT
1/3 C  BURGUNDY WINE
SEASONED SALT                          COOK AT LOW, ALL DAY
PEPPER
1 ONION, SLICED                        DRAIN (KEEPING LIQUID)


2 ONIONS, SLICED          SAUTE ONIONS UNTIL BROWNED, ADD SOUP;
BUTTER                    ADD MIXTURE TO DRAINED MEAT
1 CAN CREAM-OF-MUSHROOM SOUP   IN CROCKERY-POT; SERVE OVER
                          NOODLES
```

BEEF/ORIENTAL

```
2-3 LBS  FLANK STEAK, SLICED INTO STRIPS
2 TSP  SALT                              PUT IN
2 T    SOY SAUCE                         CROCKERY-POT
1 1/2 C  WATER

                                         COOK AT LOW,
                                         ALL DAY

1/4 C  CORN STARCH MIXED WITH
       COLD WATER (TO AVOID LUMPS)
3  ONIONS, CHOPPED                       ADD TO CROCKERY-POT;
1-2  BELL PEPPERS, IN CHUNKS             TURN TO HIGH AND COOK
4-5  TOMATOES, IN CHUNKS                 FOR 1 HOUR, OR UNTIL
3 STALKS  CELERY, IN DIAGONAL SLICES     LIQUID THICKENS


1 1/2 C  BOILING WATER              IN SAUCEPAN WITH LID,
1 C    LONG GRAIN WHITE RICE        BRING TO A BOIL, REDUCE HEAT
1 T    MARGARINE                    AND SIMMER UNTIL WATER ABSORBED

SESAME SEEDS                    SERVE MEAT AND VEGETABLES FROM
CHOPPED GREEN ONION TOPS        CROCKERY-POT OVER RICE GARNISHED
                                WITH SESAME SEEDS & ONION TOPS
```

BEEF/PICKLED

```
3-4 POUND  BEEF ROAST
2 CANS  STEWED TOMATOES          PLACE IN
1/4 C  VINEGAR                   CROCKERY-POT
1 TSP  GARLIC JUICE
4-5  WHOLE CLOVES                COOK AT LOW,
1/4 TSP  PICKLING SPICE          ALL DAY
SALT
PEPPER
1 BAY LEAF, ON TOP, FOR EASY REMOVAL
```

BEEF/POT-ROASTED, GERMAN

```
3-4 POUND  BEEF ROAST, FAT REMOVED   DREDGE IN    PLACE IN
FLOUR                                FLOUR,       CROCKERY-POT
OIL                                  BROWN IN
                                     OIL
SALT                                              COOK AT LOW,
PEPPER                                            ALL DAY
1/2 TSP  GINGER
5  WHOLE CLOVES
5  APPLES, SLICED
1  ONION, SLICED
1/2  BAY LEAF, ON TOP FOR EASY REMOVAL
1/2  C  BURGUNDY WINE
```

BEEF/POT-ROASTED, VEGETABLES

```
3-4 CARROTS, IN CHUNKS ON BOTTOM OF POT
3-4 POUND  BEEF BRISKET              PLACE IN
2    ONIONS, CHOPPED                 CROCKERY-POT
1/2 C  CELERY, CHOPPED
1/2 TSP  THYME                       COOK AT LOW,
2  TSP  SALT                         ALL DAY
PEPPER
SOY SAUCE
WORCESTERSHIRE SAUCE
POTATOES, IN CHUNKS TO FILL CROCKERY-POT
          1-INCH FROM TOP
1 BAY LEAF, ON TOP FOR EASY REMOVAL
1/2 C  BOULLION
1/2 C  BURGUNDY WINE

1/4 C  CORNSTARCH DISSOLVED IN COLD WATER,   ADD TO CROCKERY-POT,
             TO AVOID LUMPS                  CONTINUE COOKING
1 PKG  FROZEN PEAS                           30-40 MINUTES
```

18

BEEF/PRUNES

```
2-3 POUNDS   STEW MEAT
2    BELL PEPPERS, CHOPPED
2    ONIONS, CHOPPED
2 CANS   STEWED TOMATOES
1 TSP   SALT
1/4 TSP   PEPPER
1 TSP   SUGAR
10-12   DRIED PITTED PRUNES
POTATOES, IN CHUNKS TO FILL CROCKERY-POT
          1-INCH FROM TOP
```

PLACE IN
CROCKERY-POT

COOK AT LOW,
ALL DAY

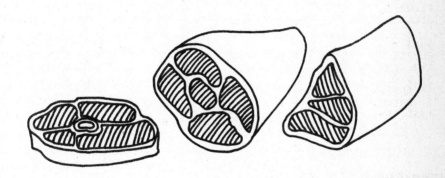

BEEF/ROAST

```
3-4 POUND   BEEF ROAST
SALT
PEPPER
1-2 ONIONS, SLICED
```

PLACE IN CROCKERY-POT, DO NOT
ADD ANY LIQUIDS

COOK AT LOW, ALL DAY

BEEF/ROAST & GRAVY

```
3-4 POUND   ROAST
SALT
PEPPER

1 ENVELOPE   ONION SOUP MIX
1 CAN   CREAM OF MUSHROOM SOUP

OR  2-3 STALKS CELERY, CHOPPED
    1 CAN   CREAM OF CELERY SOUP
```

PLACE IN CROCKERY-POT

COOK AT LOW, ALL DAY

SERVE WITH SAUCE MADE OF
SOUR CREAM BLENDED WITH
HORSERADISH SAUCE

BEEF/ROULADES

1 FLANK STEAK, CUT IN 6 PIECES,
    POUNDED THIN WITH SAUCER EDGE;
    OR, ROUND STEAK IN 6 PIECES

3/4 LB GROUND PORK, BROWNED & DRAINED
1 TSP   POULTRY SEASONING   MIX
GARLIC JUICE, OR MINCED GARLIC
1/4   ONION, MINCED
1/2   CUBE MARGARINE, MELTED
3/4 C DRY PACKAGED STUFFING MIX

PLACE IN
CROCKERY-POT

COOK AT LOW,
ALL DAY

                 DIVIDE THE STUFFING MIX ON
                 THE SIX PIECES OF BEEF, ROLL
                 AND TIE WITH COTTON TWINE

FLOUR
OIL   DREDGE IN FLOUR, BROWN IN OIL

1 BAY LEAF, ON TOP FOR EASY REMOVAL
1/2 C BURGUNDY WINE

1 BAG   FROZEN BOILING ONIONS   ADD TO CROCKERY-POT AND
1 LB   FRESH MUSHROOMS, SLICED CONTINUE COOKING 30-40 MINUTES

BEEF/ROULADES, GERMAN

1 FLANK STEAK CUT IN 4 PIECES,
    POUNDED VERY THIN WITH SAUCER EDGE
4 SLICES BACON, BROWNED & DRAINED
1 ONION, DICED

PLACE IN
CROCKERY-POT

1 LARGE DILL PICKLE, CUT LENGTHWAYS INTO
               FOUR PIECES
2 CARROTS, EACH CUT IN HALF, LENGTHWAYS
2 STALKS CELERY, EACH CUT IN HALF

COOK AT LOW,
ALL DAY

                PUT BACON & ONION ON THINNED
                FLANK STEAK PIECES, PUT ONE
                PIECE EACH OF PICKLE, CARROT,
                & CELERY ON MEAT AND ROLL;
                TIE EACH ROLL WITH COTTON TWINE

FLOUR
OIL   DREDGE WITH FLOUR, BROWN
1 ONION, SLICED   IN OIL WITH ONION SLICES

1/2 C WATER

BEEF/SAUERBRATEN

```
4-5 POUND   CHUCK ROAST,
            FAT REMOVED       MARINATE IN
1 T  SALT                     GLASS BOWL, IN
PEPPER                        REFRIGERATOR,
1/2 TSP  MSG                  FOR 2 OR 3 DAYS      COOK AT LOW,
1/4 C     BROWN SUGAR         -TURN SEVERAL        ALL DAY
2  C   WATER                  TIMES
2  C   VINEGAR                                     DRAIN THROUGH
1/2 C BURGUNDY WINE           DRAIN, STRAIN        COLANDER INTO
2  ONIONS, MINCED             THE MARINADE         LARGE SAUCEPAN,
2  BAY LEAVES                 AND PUT 1 C          RETURN MEAT TO
12 PEPPERCORNS                IN CROCKERY-POT      CROCKERY-POT
8  WHOLE CLOVES
2 T CELERY FLAKES
1/4 TSP THYME
1  TSP   DRY MUSTARD


FLOUR
OIL            DREDGE IN FLOUR, BROWN IN OIL


2 C   LIQUID FROM CROCKERY-POT
1/4 C  RAISINS                       COOK IN SAUCEPAN UNTIL
18   DARK GINGERSNAPS, CRUSHED       THICKENED, SERVE OVER MEAT
```

BEEF/SHANK

```
                              USE IN RECIPES
                              INSTEAD OF STEW MEAT
```

BEEF/SHORT RIBS

```
3-4 LBS   SHORT RIBS, FAT
          REMOVED       DREDGE IN FLOUR,    PLACE IN
FLOUR                   BROWN IN OIL        CROCKERY-POT
OIL
                                            COOK AT LOW,
SALT                                        ALL DAY
PEPPER
1/2 TSP  BAY LEAF, CRUMBLED
1  T  DRIED PARSLEY
1/2 TSP  CARAWAY SEED
3/4 C  BEER
2 BOUILLON CUBES


1 PKG   FROZEN ONIONS    ADD TO CROCKERY-POT AND CONTINUE
        IN CREAM SAUCE   COOKING 30-40 MINUTES
```

BEEF/SHORT RIBS, VEGETABLES

3-4 LBS SHORT RIBS,
     FAT REMOVED   DREDGE IN FLOUR,   PLACE IN
FLOUR   BROWN IN OIL   CROCKERY-POT
OIL

                                                     COOK AT LOW,
6 CARROTS, IN CHUNKS IN BOTTOM OF CROCKERY-POT   ALL DAY
SALT
PEPPER
2 ONIONS, CHOPPED
POTATOES, IN CHUNKS TO FILL CROCKERY-POT
       1 OR 2 INCHES FROM TOP
1 CAN STEWED TOMATOES

BEEF/SMOKED IN FOIL

BEEF BRISKET TO FIT CROCKERY POT
LARGE PIECE ALUMINUM FOIL   SEAL TIGHTLY IN
1-2 TSP LIQUID SMOKE   ALUMINUM FOIL
1 TSP GARLIC SALT
PEPPER   PLACE IN CROCKERY-POT
2 ONIONS, SLICED
1/2 C HOT BARBECUE SAUCE   COOK AT LOW, ALL DAY

BEEF/STEW

3-4 POUNDS STEW MEAT
FLOUR   DREDGE IN FLOUR,
PAPRIKA   BROWN IN OIL   PLACE IN
OIL   CROCKERY-POT

1 POTATO, IN CHUNKS   COOK AT LOW,
2 ONIONS, SLICED   ALL DAY
5-6 CARROTS, SLICED
1/2 C QUICK-COOKING TAPIOCA
2 BOULLION CUBES
1/2 TSP SEASONED SALT
PEPPER
1/2 TSP GARLIC JUICE
1 BAY LEAF, ON TOP FOR EASY REMOVAL
1 T WORCESTERSHIRE SAUCE
1 T SOY SAUCE
1/4 C BURGUNDY WINE

1 PKG FROZEN BOILING ONIONS   ADD TO CROCKERY-POT AND MIX;
1 PKG FROZEN PEAS   COOK ADDITIONAL 30-40 MINUTES

BEEF/STROGANOFF

2-3 POUNDS BEEF, CUT IN 1/2-INCH STRIPS SALT, PEPPER FLOUR OIL	DREDGE IN FLOUR AND SEASONINGS, BROWN IN OIL	PLACE IN CROCKERY-POT COOK AT LOW, ALL DAY
SALT PEPPER 1 ONION, CHOPPED 3 T TOMATO PASTE 1 BAY LEAF, CRUMBLED 1 CLOVE GARLIC, MASHED 2 BOULLION CUBES 1/2 C SHERRY		PRIOR TO SERVING, TURN OFF AND ALLOW TO COOL
2 C FRESH MUSHROOMS, SLICED BUTTER 3 T FLOUR	SAUTE, STIR INTO CROCKERY-POT	
1/2 C SOUR CREAM	ADD TO MEAT-MUSHROOM MIXTURE IN CROCKERY-POT (SOUR CREAM WILL CURDLE & SEPARATE IF ADDED TO BOILING LIQUID)	

BEEF/SWISS STEAK

2 LBS BOTTOM ROUND OR SWISS STEAK FLOUR OIL	DREDGE IN FLOUR, BROWN IN OIL	PLACE IN CROCKERY POT COOK AT LOW, ALL DAY
2 ONIONS, SLICED 2 STALKS CELERY, SLICED 1 CARROT, DICED 1 TOMATO, CHOPPED 1/2 BELL PEPPER, DICED 1/2 TSP GARLIC JUICE 1 T WORCESTERSHIRE SAUCE SALT, PEPPER 1 TSP OREGANO 1 TSP THYME 1 TSP CUMIN 1 C TOMATO PUREE 1/4 C CORNSTARCH DISSOLVED IN COLD WATER		

23

BEEF/TONGUE

1 BEEF TONGUE	
1 ONION, QUARTERED	PLACE IN CROCKERY-POT
1 CARROT, DICED	
1/2 BAY LEAF	COOK AT LOW, ALL DAY
SALT	
PEPPER	REMOVE FROM CROCKERY-POT WITH A FORK,
1 C BOULLION	PEEL SKIN, TRIM GRISTLE

SERVE WITH SAUCE OF 1/2 CAN CREAM OF
MUSHROOM SOUP & HORSERADISH

BEEF/TONGUE, PICKLED

1 BEEF TONGUE	PLACE IN CROCKERY-POT
1/2 C DARK BROWN SUGAR, FIRMLY PACKED	
2 ONIONS, QUARTERED	COOK AT LOW, ALL DAY
SALT	
PEPPER	REMOVE FROM POT WITH
1 TSP DRY MUSTARD	FORK, PEEL SKIN AND
1/2 TSP GROUND CLOVES	TRIM GRISTLE
1/4 C VINEGAR	
1 C WATER	

BELL PEPPERS/STUFFED

6-8 BELL PEPPERS, TO FIT CROCKERY-POT	REMOVE STEM AND SEEDS; PARBOIL	STUFF PEPPERS WITH RICE-MEAT MIXTURE
1 PKG SEASONED RICE MIX, COOKED		
1 LB SAUSAGE & HAMBURGER, BROWNED & DRAINED		PUT INTO POT, IN LAYERS
1/2 ONION, CHOPPED		
1 T DRIED PARSLEY		ADD LIQUIDS
SEASONED SALT		
PEPPER		
1 (8-OUNCE) CAN TOMATO SAUCE		COOK AT LOW,
1 CAN WATER, OR BOULLION		ALL DAY

24

BREAD/BANANA

3/4 C MARGARINE, MELTED		
1 1/2 C SUGAR	COMBINED	

1 1/2 C BANANA, MASHED
2 EGGS, BEATEN
1 TSP VANILLA
2 C FLOUR
1 TSP BAKING SODA
3/4 TSP SALT
1/2 C BUTTERMILK, OR MILK
3/4 C WALNUTS, CHOPPED

POUR BATTER INTO
GREASED, FLOURED
COFFEE CAN, OR MOLD,
WHICH FITS LOOSELY IN
CROCKERY-POT

IMPORTANT: FILL ONLY
2/3 FULL

COVER TOP OF CAN WITH
5 PAPER TOWELS

DO NOT ADD WATER

PUT ON CROCKERY-POT
LID SLIGHTLY CROOKED,
SO EXCESS MOISTURE CAN
ESCAPE

COOK ON HIGH, 4 HOURS

BREAD/BROWN

1 C WHOLE WHEAT FLOUR
1 C CORNMEAL
1 TSP BAKING POWDER
1 TSP BAKING SODA
1/2 TSP SALT
1/2 C DARK MOLASSES
1 1/2 C SOUR MILK, OR
          BUTTERMILK
1 C NUTS, CHOPPED
1 C RAISINS / DATES

POUR BATTER INTO GREASED, FLOURED
COFFEE CAN, OR MOLD, WHICH FITS LOOSELY
IN CROCKERY-POT

FILL ONLY 2/3 FULL

COVER CAN TOP TIGHTLY WITH FOIL

PLACE CAN IN CROCKERY-POT

POUR 1-1/2 C WATER BETWEEN CAN AND SIDE
OF CROCKERY-POT, DO NOT FILL ABOVE
1/2-INCH FROM TOP

PUT FOIL OVER TOP OF CROCKERY-POT, PUT
LID ON POT (OVER THE FOIL)

COOK AT HIGH, APPROXIMATELY 4 HOURS

25

BURRITO

3-4 POUNDS STEW MEAT	
1 CAN CHILI SALSA	PLACE IN CROCKERY-POT
SALT	
PEPPER	COOK AT LOW, ALL DAY
1 T CHILI POWDER	

1 LARGE CAN CHILI BEANS	ADD TO CROCKERY-POT, HEAT FOR 30-45 MINUTES

LARGE FLOUR TORTILLAS, WARMED IN OVEN TO SOFTEN	WRAP ALL INGREDIENTS IN SOFTENED TORTILLAS, TOP WITH
CHEDDAR CHEESE, GRATED	ADDITIONAL MEAT-BEAN MIX,
ONION, CHOPPED	CHEESE, AND GARNISH WITH CHOPPED GREEN ONION TOPS

CABBAGE/GERMAN

CABBAGE, DICED, TO FILL CROCKERY-POT

3 T BACON GREASE		COOK AT LOW,
1 C HOT WATER	COMBINE AND	ALL DAY
1 1/2 TSP SALT	POUR OVER	
1/2 TSP PEPPER	CABBAGE IN	
1 T SUGAR	CROCKERY-POT	
1/2 C VINEGAR		

CABBAGE/ROLLS, GERMAN

CABBAGE, PARBOILED TO SOFTEN AND SEPARATE LEAVES

		PLACE IN
1 PKG SEASONED RICE, COOKED	FILL EACH	CROCKERY-POT
1/2 LB SAUSAGE, BROWNED & DRAINED	SOFTENED	IN LAYERS
1/2 LB HAMBURGER, BROWNED & DRAINED	LEAF WITH	
1 ONION, CHOPPED	MEAT-RICE	
1/2 TSP GARLIC JUICE	MIXTURE	
1/2 TSP SALT	AND ROLL	
PEPPER		
2 EGGS		
1 SMALL CAN SAUERKRAUT		

BROWN SUGAR	SPRINKLE SUGAR OVER
2 (6-OUNCE) CANS SEASONED TOMATO SAUCE	EACH LAYER OF CABBAGE ROLLS; ADD TOMATO SAUCE
	COOK AT LOW, ALL DAY

26

CABBAGE/ROLLS, GREEK

CABBAGE, PARBOILED TO SOFTEN AND SEPARATE LEAVES

1 LB GROUND LAMB, BROWNED & DRAINED		PLACE CABBAGE
1 LB HAMBURGER, BROWNED & DRAINED	FILL	ROLLS IN
1 T OLIVE OIL	EACH	LAYERS IN
1 ONION, CHOPPED	LEAF	CROCKERY-POT
1 TOMATO, DICED	WITH	
1/2 C BROWN MINUTE RICE, UNCOOKED	MEAT	ADD BOULLION
1 TSP SALT	MIX-	
PEPPER	TURE,	COOK AT LOW,
1 T DRIED PARSLEY	AND	ALL DAY
1 TSP DRIED MINT	ROLL	

1 CAN BEEF BROTH (BOULLION)

1 C LIQUID FROM CROCKERY-POT, BOILING IN SAUCEPAN	BOIL, STIRRING
2 T CORNSTARCH DISSOLVED IN COLD WATER TO AVOID LUMPS	CONSTANTLY, TO THICKEN

3 EGGS, BEATEN FLUFFY	
1/4 C LEMON JUICE	ADD SLOWLY TO THICKENED LIQUID;
SALT	SERVE AS SAUCE OVER CABBAGE ROLLS

CABBAGE/STUFFED

1 CABBAGE TO FIT CROCKERY-POT,
    WITH CENTER HOLLOWED-OUT
    FOR STUFFING
		PLACE WHOLE
		STUFFED
		CABBAGE IN

1/2 LB HOT SAUSAGE, BROWNED & DRAINED		CROCKERY-POT
1/2 LB HAMBURGER, BROWNED & DRAINED	STUFF	
1 EGG	CABBAGE	ADD LIQUID
1 ONION, CHOPPED		
1 T DRIED PARSLEY		COOK AT LOW,
1 TSP GARLIC SALT		ALL DAY
PEPPER		

1 CAN   BEEF BROTH (BOULLION)

1/2 PINT SOUR CREAM	IN SAUCEPAN,
1/2 C LIQUID FROM CROCKERY-POT	HEAT, BUT DO NOT BOIL
2 T TOMATO PASTE	(SOUR CREAM WILL CURDLE
GARLIC SALT	IF BOILED); SERVE SAUCE
PEPPER	OVER CABBAGE WITH WIDE NOODLES

27

CAKE/APPLE

1 CUBE MARGARINE, MELTED		POUR BATTER INTO GREASED,
2 EGGS	CREAM	FLOURED COFFEE CAN, OR
1 C SUGAR	TOGETHER	MOLD, WHICH FITS LOOSELY
1/4 C WATER		IN CROCKERY-POT

1 1/4 C FLOUR, SIFTED
1 T COCOA
1/2 TSP BAKING SODA
1/2 TSP CINNAMON
1/2 TSP ALLSPICE

IMPORTANT: FILL ONLY 2/3

1/2 C WALNUTS, CHOPPED
1/3 C CHOCOLATE DROPS
1 C GRATED APPLES
1 TSP VANILLA
1/4 C RAISINS OR CHOPPED DATES

COVER TOP OF CAN WITH
5 PAPER TOWELS

DO NOT ADD WATER

PUT ON CROCKERY-POT LID
SLIGHTLY CROOKED, SO
EXCESS MOISTURE CAN
ESCAPE

CAKE/APPLESAUCE

COOK ON HIGH,
APPROXIMATELY 4 HOURS

1 CUBE MARGARINE, MELTED		
1 C SUGAR	CREAM	
2 T WATER	TOGETHER	

1 1/2 C APPLESAUCE
2 C FLOUR
2 TSP BAKING SODA
1 TSP CINNAMON
1/2 TSP CLOVES
1/2 TSP ALLSPICE
1 C RAISINS

FOLLOW DIRECTIONS ABOVE

CAKE/CARROT

1 C SUGAR
1/3 C SALAD OIL
2 EGGS
1/3 C BUTTERMILK
1 TSP VANILLA
1 1/4 C FLOUR
1/2 TSP BAKING SODA
1/4 TSP SALT
1 TSP CINNAMON
1/2 TSP NUTMEG
1/2 TSP CLOVES
1 C GRATED CARROTS
1/2 C NUTS, CHOPPED
1/3 C CANNED CRUSHED PINEAPPLE,
       SQUEEZED DRY
1/2 C CHOPPED DATES OR RAISINS

FOLLOW DIRECTIONS ABOVE

```
1 1/2 C RAISINS          SIMMER TO PLUMP RAISINS;
2   C   SHERRY WINE      DRAIN, KEEPING LIQUID


1/2 C SHORTENING (CRISCO)
3/4 C SUGAR                   CREAM        POUR BATTER INTO GREASED,
                                           FLOURED COFFEE CAN, OR
1 EGG                                      MOLD, WHICH FITS LOOSELY
3/4 C + 2 T LIQUID DRAINED                 IN CROCKERY-POT
            FROM RAISINS
1 1/2 C   FLOUR                            IMPORTANT: FILL ONLY 2/3
1 TSP   BAKING POWDER
1/2 TSP   SALT                             COVER TOP OF CAN WITH
1   TSP   CINNAMON                         5 PAPER TOWELS
1/2 TSP   NUTMEG
1   C     WALNUTS, CHOPPED                 DO NOT ADD WATER
RAISINS, PLUMPED AND CHOPPED
                                           PUT ON CROCKERY-POT LID
                                           SLIGHTLY CROOKED, SO
1 CUBE BUTTER OR                           EXCESS MOISTURE CAN
  MARGARINE AT           CREAM             ESCAPE
  ROOM TEMPERATURE       TO MAKE
4 T   SHERRY            SAUCE              COOK ON HIGH,
POWDERED SUGAR, AS       FOR               APPROXIMATELY 4 HOURS
  NEEDED                 CAKE
```

```
1 PKG   WHITE CAKE MIX      OR   1 PKG YELLOW CAKE
1 PKG   STRAWBERRY JELLO         1 PKG LEMON JELLO        FOLLOW
4   EGGS                         4   EGGS                 BAKING
1/2 C  SALAD OIL                 1/2 C  SALAD OIL         DIRECTIONS
1/2 C  WATER                     3/4 C  WATER             ABOVE FOR
1/2 (10-OUNCE) PKG               PINCH OF SALT            EGGNOG
    FROZEN STRAWBERRIES          1 TSP LEMON EXTRACT      CAKE


1/2 CUBE SWEET BUTTER            1/2 CUBE BUTTER
    OR MARGARINE, AT       OR    1/4 C   LEMON JUICE      CREAM TO
    ROOM TEMPERATURE             POWDERED SUGAR           MAKE SAUCE
1/2 PKG  STRAWBERRIES                                     FOR CAKE
POWDERED SUGAR, AS
  NEEDED
```

29

CHEESE/WELSH RABBIT

2 LBS   SHARP CHEDDAR CHEESE, GRATED
1/2 TSP   GARLIC SALT
1/2 TSP   CELERY SALT
1/4 TSP   PEPPER
1   TSP   PAPRIKA
DASH MSG
2   TSP   DRY MUSTARD
1/4 TSP   ONION POWDER
3   TSP   CORNSTARCH
1   T   WORCESTERSHIRE SAUCE
1 1/2 CANS   BEER
1   CAN   TOMATO SOUP
1   CLOVE GARLIC, CRUSHED
4   EGG YOLKS, BEATEN & ADDED AFTER
            CHEESE IS MELTED

PUT INTO CROCKERY-POT
IN ORDER LISTED, MIXING
"DRY" INGREDIENTS BEFORE
ADDING LIQUIDS

COOK AT LOW, 2 TO 6
HOURS

SERVE OVER TOAST, OR AS
FONDUE WITH CUBES OF
SOURDOUGH BREAD

CHICKEN/BRAISED

2 CHICKENS, WITH ALL POSSIBLE FAT REMOVED
    (IF DIETING, REMOVE SKIN ALSO)
SALT
PEPPER   SEASON CHICKEN INSIDE & OUT
PAPRIKA

1 ENVELOPE CHICKEN GRAVY MIX
2 CARROTS, SLICED
2 STALKS CELERY, SLICED
1 ONION, SLICED
1 C   WHITE WINE

PLACE WHOLE
CHICKENS IN
CROCKERY-POT
WITH VEGETABLES
AND WINE

COOK AT LOW,
4-6 HOURS

BROTH MAY BE
THICKENED WITH
CORNSTARCH

CHICKEN/BREASTS, GRAVY

8 CHICKEN BREASTS
SALT
PEPPER
1 CAN CREAM OF MUSHROOM SOUP
1/4 C SHERRY, OR WHITE WINE

PLACE IN CROCKERY-POT

COOK AT LOW, 4-6 HOURS

1 LB FRESH MUSHROOMS, SLICED
BUTTER

SAUTE, STIR INTO CROCKERY-POT;
TURN OFF POT, TO COOL

1 C   SOUR CREAM   ADD TO CHICKEN-MUSHROOM MIXTURE IN CROCKERY-
                          POT (SOUR CREAM WILL CURDLE AND SEPARATE IF
                          ADDED TO BOILING LIQUID)

CHICKEN/CACCIATORA

3 POUNDS CHICKEN PARTS
2 CLOVES GARLIC, CRUSHED | BROWN, DRAIN | PLACE IN CROCKERY-
1/4 C OLIVE OIL | | POT

1 TSP SALT | COOK AT LOW,
PEPPER | 4-6 HOURS
1 TSP PAPRIKA |
2 TSP OREGANO | SERVE WITH BUTTERED
1/2 TSP BASIL | SPAGHETTI
1/2 TSP ROSEMARY |
1 ONION, MINCED |
1 CAN STEWED TOMATOES |
1/4 C SAUTERNE WINE |

CHICKEN/CHILI

10-12 CHICKEN PARTS

| BRUSH EACH CHICKEN PIECE
1 ENVL. CHILI SEASONING MIX | WITH CHILI
1/4 C VINEGAR |
GARLIC SALT | SEAL EACH PIECE TIGHTLY
PEPPER | IN ALUMINUM FOIL
2 T ONION, GRATED |

PLACE PACKETS IN CROCKERY-POT

COOK AT LOW, 4-6 HOURS

CHICKEN/CURRY

4 LBS CHICKEN PARTS
1/2 ONION, MINCED | PLACE IN CROCKERY-POT;
SALT, PEPPER | COOK AT LOW, 4-6 HOURS
1 CLOVE GARLIC, CRUSHED |
1 TSP CURRY POWDER | DRAIN; ALLOW TO COOL, THEN REMOVE
| MEAT AND DISCARD BONES

2 CANS CREAM/MUSHROOM SOUP
1 CAN BROTH FROM CROCKERY-POT | HEAT IN SAUCEPAN TO BLEND
SALT | FLAVORS, ADD BONED MEAT FROM
CURRY TO TASTE | CROCKERY-POT; SERVE OVER
COOKED CHICKEN | WHITE RICE

1 LB DICED BACON, BROWNED & DRAINED
1 ONION, CHOPPED | SERVE WITH CHICKEN
BOILED EGGS, CHOPPED | CURRY AS CONDIMENTS
GREEN ONION TOPS, CHOPPED | IN INDIVIDUAL SERVING
WALNUTS, CHOPPED | DISHES
RAISINS
CHUTNEY

CHICKEN/GIZZARDS, GRAVY

```
3 POUNDS  GIZZARDS AND HEARTS, SLICED
1/4  ONION, MINCED                         PLACE IN CROCKERY-POT
1/4  CARROT, GRATED
1 STALK CELERY, MINCED                     COOK AT LOW, ALL DAY
1/4 TSP  SALT
PEPPER
1 C  WATER


1/2 C  LIQUID FROM CROCKERY-POT
1 CAN  CREAM OF MUSHROOM SOUP              ADD TO CROCKERY-POT,
1 PKG  FROZEN ONIONS IN CREAM SAUCE        CONTINUE COOKING
SALT, PEPPER                               APPROXIMATELY 30 MINUTES
```

CHICKEN/GIZZARDS, SHERRY

```
3 POUNDS  GIZZARDS, SLICED     PLACE IN CROCKERY-POT
1/4  ONION, MINCED
1/4  CARROT, GRATED            COOK AT LOW, ALL DAY
1/2  STALK CELERY, MINCED
1 C  WATER                     DRAIN, RESERVING LIQUID


1 LARGE ONION, SLICED    SAUTE IN LARGE
BUTTER, OR MARGARINE     SAUCEPAN                    SERVE OVER
                                                     FLUFFY WHITE RICE
COOKED GIZZARDS
2 C  SHERRY
3-4 CANS WHOLE BUTTON MUSHROOMS, DRAINED
2 C  LIQUID FROM CROCKERY-POT, STRAINED
GARLIC OIL, TO TASTE
2 T  DISSOLVED IN COLD WATER, TO
     AVOID LUMPS
SALT, PEPPER
```

32

CHICKEN/GRAVY

1 STEWING CHICKEN, CUT-UP
2 C WATER   PLACE IN CROCKERY-POT
1 ONION, CHOPPED
1 CARROT, SLICED   COOK AT LOW, 4-6 HOURS
2 STALKS CELERY, SLICED
1 T DRIED PARSLEY   DRAIN THROUGH COLANDER
1/2 TSP THYME   INTO LARGE SAUCEPAN,
3 TSP SALT   LEAVING CHICKEN IN
1/2 TSP PEPPER   CROCKERY-POT
2 CLOVES GARLIC, MASHED
1 BAY LEAF, ON TOP FOR EASY REMOVAL

3 T BUTTER, MELTED IN SAUCEPAN
1/4 C FLOUR, ADDED TO BUTTER   SERVE THIS SAUCE OVER
                                              CHICKEN WITH RICE OR
2 C LIQUID FROM CROCKERY-POT, STRAINED   BUTTERED NOODLES
1 C HALF-AND-HALF
1 EGG YOLK
1/2 TSP SALT
1/4 TSP PEPPER
1 TSP WORCESTERSHIRE SAUCE
1/4 TSP NUTMEG

CHICKEN/GREEK

1 ROASTING CHICKEN, WHOLE
SALT   PLACE IN CROCKERY-POT
PEPPER
OREGANO   COOK AT LOW, 4-6 HOURS
1/4 C FRESH MINT, INSIDE CHICKEN
3 LEMON SLICES, INSIDE CHICKEN   DRAIN, RESERVING LIQUID
1/2 C WHITE WINE
1 CAN   CHICKEN BROTH   SERVE WITH RICE PILAF;
2 T LEMON JUICE   RECIPE BELOW

1   ONION, SLICED THINLY   BROWN IN
1   CLOVE GARLIC, MASHED   LARGE   BRING TO
1/2 CUBE BUTTER   SAUCEPAN   BOIL;   SERVE RICE
                                           COVER AND   PILAF WITH
2 C LIQUID FROM CROCKERY-POT   SIMMER   CHICKEN
1 C RICE   UNTIL
1/2 TSP SALT   DONE
1/4 TSP PEPPER
1 T DRIED PARSLEY

1/4 C RAISINS
1/4 C PINE NUTS

33

CHICKEN/HAM

```
1 C  HAM, DICED
1 CHICKEN, CUT-UP                    PLACE IN CROCKERY-POT.
1 ONION, CHOPPED
1 BELL PEPPER, CHOPPED               COOK AT LOW, 4-6 HOURS
1 CLOVES GARLIC, MASHED
1 CAN BEEF BROTH (BOULLION)
1 CAN STEWED TOMATOES               SERVE WITH RICE MIXED WITH
1 CAN PIMENTO, DICED                COOKED FROZEN PEAS
1/2 TSP CHILI POWDER
SALT, PEPPER
```

CHICKEN/OLIVES

```
2 CHICKENS, CUT-UP       DREDGE IN
FLOUR                    FLOUR, AND
1 CLOVE GARLIC, MASHED   BROWN IN     PLACE IN CROCKERY-POT
OIL                      OIL
                                      COOK AT LOW, 4-6 HOURS
1 ONION, CHOPPED
1 CLOVE GARLIC, MASHED                SAUCE MAY BE THICKENED
2 CANS TOMATO SAUCE                   WITH CORNSTARCH DISSOLVED
1/2 C  SHERRY                         IN COLD WATER,TO AVOID
1/2 C  WATER                          LUMPS
2 CHICKEN BOULLION CUBES
SALT, PEPPER

1/2 C STUFFED OLIVES, SLICED      STIR INTO CROCKERY-POT
1 CAN SLICED MUSHROOMS, DRAINED   JUST BEFORE SERVING
```

CHICKEN/ORANGE JUICE

```
1 CHICKEN, CUT-UP    BROWN IN OIL,
OIL                  DRAIN WELL       PLACE IN CROCKERY-POT

1/2 C ORANGE JUICE                    COOK AT LOW, 4-6 HOURS
2 T  BROWN SUGAR
1/4 TSP GINGER                        SERVE WITH BROWN RICE;
2 CARDAMON SEEDS, CRUSHED; OR         RECIPE BELOW
     A PINCH OF GROUND CARDAMON
1 ENVL  CHICKEN GRAVY MIX
SALT, PEPPER


SLIVERED ALMONDS
THIN ORANGE SLICES      GARNISH CHICKEN SERVED WITH BROWN RICE

1 1/2 C LIQUID FROM CROCKERY-POT    BRING TO BOIL IN SAUCEPAN;
1 C  QUICK-COOKING BROWN RICE       COVER, REDUCE HEAT AND SIMMER
1/2 TSP SALT                        UNTIL DONE
```

CHICKEN/PAPRIKA

1 ROASTING CHICKEN, CUT-UP		PLACE IN CROCKERY-POT
FLOUR	DREDGE IN	
SALT	FLOUR, AND	COOK AT LOW, 4-6
PEPPER	BROWN IN	HOURS
OIL	OIL	
2 ONIONS, CHOPPED		TURN-OFF CROCKERY-POT
1 C RICE		A FEW MINUTES BEFORE
1 CAN CHICKEN BROTH		READY TO SERVE
1 CLOVE GARLIC, MASHED		
1 TSP SALT		
2 T SWEET PAPRIKA		
1 C SOUR CREAM	STIR INTO COOLED CROCKERY-POT	

CHICKEN/SEASONED, CURRY

2 CHICKENS, CUT-UP		PLACE IN CROCKERY-POT
FLOUR	DREDGE IN	
SALT	FLOUR, AND	COOK AT LOW, 4-6 HOURS
PEPPER	BROWN IN	
OIL	OIL	SERVE OVER RICE
1 ONION, CHOPPED		
1 BELL PEPPER, CHOPPED		
1 CLOVE GARLIC, MASHED		
3 TSP CURRY POWDER		
1/2 C RAISINS		
1 CAN STEWED TOMATOES		

CHICKEN/SEASONED, ITALIAN

1 CHICKEN, CUT-UP	
1 CAN CREAM OF MUSHROOM SOUP	PLACE IN CROCKERY-POT
1 ENVL ITALIAN SALAD DRESSING MIX	
SEASONED SALT	COOK AT LOW, 4-6 HOURS
PEPPER	
1/2 C SOUR CREAM	ADD TO CROCKERY-POT,
1 CAN MUSHROOMS, DRAINED	SERVE OVER RICE OR NOODLES

CHICKEN/STEW

1 CHICKEN, CUT-UP		
FLOUR	DREDGE IN	PLACE IN CROCKERY-POT
SALT, PEPPER	FLOUR, AND	
OIL	BROWN IN OIL	COOK AT LOW, 4-6 HOURS

1/4 LB DICED BACON, BROWNED, DRAINED
1 ONION, CHOPPED
3-4 CARROTS, SLICED
2 STALKS CELERY, SLICED
1 CAN CREAM OF MUSHROOM SOUP
1 TSP WORCESTERSHIRE SAUCE
1 CLOVE GARLIC, MINCED
SALT, PEPPER

1 PKG . FROZEN PEAS   ADD TO CROCKERY-POT, CONTINUE COOKING 30-40 MINUTES BEFORE SERVING

CHICKEN/TETRAZZINI

3-4 C COOKED CHICKEN, DICED	
2 C CHICKEN BROTH	PLACE IN CROCKERY-POT
1/2 C DRY WHITE WINE	
1 C HALF-AND-HALF	COOK AT LOW, 4-6 HOURS
1 CAN CREAM OF MUSHROOM SOUP	
1/2 - 1 LB FRESH MUSHROOMS, SLICED	

SPAGHETTI, COOKED & BUTTERED, PUT IN	PLACE UNDER BROILER
GREASED BAKING DISH	UNTIL PARMESAN CHEESE
CROCKERY-POT MIXTURE	BROWNS
3/4 C PARMESAN CHEESE , ON TOP	

CHICKEN/WINE

2 CHICKENS, CUT-UP		
2 CLOVES GARLIC, MASHED	BROWN,	PLACE IN CROCKERY-POT
OIL	DRAIN WELL	
		COOK AT LOW, 4-6 HOURS

12 SMALL WHITE ONIONS
1 C FRESH MUSHROOMS, SLICED
1/2 C DRY WHITE WINE
1 CAN CHICKEN BROTH
1 TSP SALT
1/4 TSP PEPPER
1 T DRIED PARSLEY
DASH THYME
1 BAY LEAF, CRUSHED

CHILI/MEAT SAUCE

1/2 LB CUBED SALT PORK, BROWNED, DRAINED	
2 LBS BEEF STEW MEAT, DICED,BROWNED,DRAINED	PLACE IN
1 CAN BEEF BROTH (BOULLION)	CROCKERY-POT
2 CANS TOMATO SAUCE	
3 T DRIED GARLIC	COOK AT LOW,
3 TSP GROUND CUMIN	ALL DAY
1 T SALT	
1/2 TSP CAYENNE PEPPER	SERVE OVER WARM
4-6 T CHILI POWDER	CANNED KIDNEY
1/4 C CORN FLOUR (NOT CORNMEAL)	BEANS, ONIONS

CRAB/SHERRY

1 POUND FRESH OR FROZEN CRAB MEAT,	
LOBSTER, OR SHRIMP	PLACE IN CROCKERY-POT
1/4 CUBE BUTTER	
1/4 C HALF-AND-HALF	COOK ON LOW, 4 TO 6 HOURS
1 CAN CREAM OF MUSHROOM SOUP	- DO NOT OVERCOOK
1/4 C SHERRY	
1 EGG	
1/4 ONION, MINCED	
1/2 TSP WORCESTERSHIRE SAUCE	
1 T DRIED PARSLEY	
SALT, PEPPER	

INDIVIDUAL PIE SHELLS, BAKED	PUT COOKED CRAB IN PIE SHELLS
PARMESAN CHEESE	AND GARNISH WITH CHEESE AND
PAPRIKA	SEASONINGS; BROIL UNTIL GOLDEN
NUTMEG	

DIP/CHEESE

1 (10-OUNCE) CAN CHEESE SAUCE	
1 POUND MILD CHEDDAR CHEESE, GRATED	MIX IN CROCKERY-
1 (4-OUNCE) CAN GREEN CHILES, DICED	POT; HEAT AT LOW,
OR, USE CHILI SALSA , WHICH IS MILDER	1 OR 2 HOURS
SALT	
PEPPER	SERVE WITH CORN
PAPRIKA, TO TASTE	CHIPS; OR RAW
	VEGETABLES, SLICED

37

DRINKS/CHOCOLATE

```
1/2 C   COCOA
3/4 C   SUGAR
PINCH SALT
1/4 TSP   CINNAMON
1/4 TSP   VANILLA
1/4 CUBE   BUTTER
2   T   FLOUR
8   C   MILK
2   C   WATER
```

COOK IN CROCKERY-POT ON HIGH FOR 1 HOUR,
TURN TO LOW UNTIL READY TO SERVE WITH
WHIPPED CREAM OR MARSHMALLOWS

DRINKS/CIDER

```
8 C   SWEET APPLE CIDER
3/4 C   BROWN SUGAR, FIRMLY PACKED
DASH SALT
2 TSP   CINNAMON
1 TSP   CLOVES, GROUND
1 TSP   ALLSPICE
1/2 TSP   NUTMEG, GROUND
```

HEAT IN CROCKERY-POT AT
LOW; 2 HOURS, OR LONGER

DRINKS/WASSAIL

```
6 C   SWEET APPLE CIDER
1 1/2   C   CRANBERRY JUICE
1/2 C   BROWN SUGAR, FIRMLY PACKED
1/4 C   GRANULATED SUGAR
2   TSP   CINNAMON
1   TSP   ALLSPICE
1   TSP   CLOVES, GROUND
1/2 TSP NUTMEG, GROUND
1   ORANGE, THINLY SLICED
```

HEAT IN CROCKERY-POT AT
LOW; 2 HOURS, OR LONGER

DRINKS/WINE, MULLED

```
2 FIFTHS   BURGUNDY WINE, OR COMBINE
             BURGUNDY & PORT, OR SHERRY
1/4 - 1/2 C   BRANDY
2 LEMONS, THINLY SLICED
1/2 C   FRESH LEMON JUICE
1 ORANGE, THINLY SLICED
1/3 C   RAISINS
3 STICKS   CINNAMON
20 WHOLE CLOVES
3/4 C   SUGAR
1/4 C SLIVERED ALMONDS, TOASTED UNDER BROILER
```

HEAT IN CROCKERY-
POT; 2 HOURS,
OR LONGER

ENCHILADAS

3-4 POUNDS STEW MEAT	
1 CAN CHILI SALSA	PLACE IN CROCKERY-POT
SALT	
PEPPER	COOK AT LOW, ALL DAY
1 T CHILI POWDER	
1 CAN REFRIED BEANS	
1 ONION, CHOPPED	ADD TO COOKED MEAT MIXTURE IN
1/4 TSP GARLIC POWDER	CROCKERY-POT; MIX, CONTINUE
1/4 TSP CUMIN	COOKING
1 CAN SLICED OLIVES, DRAINED	
TACO SAUCE, TO TASTE	
HOT OIL, IN LARGE SKILLET	FRY EACH TORTILLA QUICKLY, JUST
CORN TORTILLAS	TO SOFTEN; DRAIN WELL ON PAPER
	TOWELS
2 (10-OUNCE) CANS ENCHILADA	DIP EACH SOFTENED TORTILLA IN
SAUCE IN FLAT DISH	SAUCE, FILL WITH MEAT-BEAN MIX
	FROM CROCKERY-POT
	PLACE ROLLED ENCHILADAS IN
	GREASED BAKING DISH, SEAM DOWN
	POUR ON REMAINING ENCHILADA SAUCE
1 POUND CHEDDAR CHEESE,	
GRATED	ADD CHEESE, BAKE 20-30 MINUTES
	IN 375° OVEN
1 CAN SLICED OLIVES, DRAINED	
SOUR CREAM	GARNISH JUST BEFORE SERVING
GREEN ONION TOPS, CHOPPED	

FISH/BOULLIBAISSE

OLIVE OIL, IN SKILLET		
2 ONIONS, SLICED		
1 CARROT, SLICED THINLY		
1 STALK CELERY, SLICED	SAUTE UNTIL	PLACE IN CROCKERY-POT
2 CLOVES GARLIC, MASHED	LIMP	
		COOK AT LOW, 2 TO 4
1 (16-OUNCE) CAN TOMATOES		HOURS
1 CAN TOMATO SAUCE		
1 BAY LEAF		
SALT, PEPPER		
1 T PAPRIKA		
2 T LEMON JUICE		
1/2 C SHERRY		
2 C WATER		
1 LB FRESH OR FROZEN SHRIMP		ADD TO CROCKERY-POT
1 LB FRESH OR FROZEN CRAB		
1 LB FRESH OR FROZEN LOBSTER		CONTINUE COOKING, AT
2 LB FRESH OR FROZEN HALIBUT, CUBED		LOW, 2 TO 3 HOURS
1 DOZEN FRESH OYSTERS, CLAMS, OR SCALLOPS		

39

FONDUE/CHOCOLATE

6 (1-OUNCE) SQUARES SEMI-SWEET CHOCOLATE
1 CUBE   BUTTER
1 1/2 C SUGAR
PINCH SALT
1/4 C HALF-AND-HALF
FLAVOR TO TASTE WITH: VANILLA EXTRACT
                OR ALMOND EXTRACT
                    CREME DE COCOA
                    RUM

PLACE IN CROCKERY-POT
AND STIR OCCASIONALLY

HEAT AT LOW FOR 2
HOURS, OR LONGER

DOUGHNUTS, CUT IN BITE-SIZE PIECES
ANGEL FOOD CAKE, CUBED
MARSHMALLOWS
APPLES, CUBED
BANANAS, IN CHUNKS
FROZEN BANANAS, IN CHUNKS
FRESH PEACHES, CUBED

SERVE WITH FONDUE FORKS
FOR DIPPING INTO WARM
CHOCOLATE MIXTURE

FRUIT/DRIED, MARSHMALLOWS

1 1/2 C DRIED APRICOTS OR PRUNES
PINCH OF SALT
1 1/2 C WATER

PLACE IN CROCKERY-POT

COOK AT LOW, ALL DAY

24 MARSHMALLOWS
WHIPPED CREAM
MARASCHINO CHERRIES

MIX MARSHMALLOWS INTO FRUIT AND PARTIALLY
MELT, WHIP WITH A FORK
SERVE WARM OR COLD WITH WHIPPED CREAM
                        AND CHERRY GARNISH

FRUIT/DRIED, MIXED

1 (8-OUNCE) PKG DRIED APRICOTS, CHOPPED
1 (16-OUNCE) PKG PITTED DRIED PRUNES, CHOPPED
1/2 C RAISINS, SEEDLESS AND/OR MUSKAT
1 (20-OUNCE) CAN PINEAPPLE CHUNKS, WITH JUICE
1 CAN   PITTED DARK SWEET CHERRIES, WITH JUICE
1/4 C   BRANDY
1/4 C   PORT WINE
1 C   WATER

PUT IN CROCKERY-
POT AND MIX

COOK AT LOW 2-4
HOURS; BECOMES
SOMEWHAT SOUR IF
COOKED LONGER AND
SUGAR MUST BE
ADDED

GAME HENS/STUFFED

1 (6-1/2 OUNCE) BAG DRY STUFFING MIX
1 CUBE BUTTER, OR MARGARINE, MELTED
1 ONION, MINCED
1-2 APPLES, CHOPPED
1/2 C RAISINS
WALNUTS, OR SLIVERED ALMONDS
1 T DRIED PARSLEY
SEASONED SALT
PEPPER
2 T SHERRY
LIQUID TO MOISTEN: ORANGE JUICE
                 AND/OR CHICKEN BROTH
                         WATER

MIX AND STUFF INTO
SALTED GAME HENS

SEAL EACH HEN TIGHTLY
IN FOIL, SEAL EXCESS
DRESSING IN ANOTHER
FOIL PACKET

PLACE SEALED HENS IN
CROCKERY-POT, PLACE
DRESSING PACKET ON TOP

COOK AT LOW, ALL DAY

GREEN BEANS

1/2 LB DICED BACON, BROWNED, DRAINED
2-3 LBS FRESH GREEN BEANS, CUT-UP
1 TSP SALT
3 C WATER

PLACE IN CROCKERY-POT

COOK AT LOW, ALL DAY

HAM/FRUIT SAUCE

3-4 LBS PRECOOKED HAM,OR THICK HAM SLICES
1/2 C BROWN SUGAR, FIRMLY PACKED
1/2 C RAISINS, MUSCAT OR SEEDLESS
1 CAN SLICED PINEAPPLE, DRAINED
1/2 TSP GROUND CLOVES
1/4 C ORANGE JUICE
1/2 C APPLE CIDER
1/2 C PORT WINE

PLACE IN CROCKERY-
POT

COOK AT LOW, ALL
DAY

HAM/GREEN BEANS

2-3 POUND PRECOOKED HAM
2 POUNDS FRESH GREEN BEANS, CUT-UP
1 ONION, DICED
GARLIC SALT
PEPPER
2 C WATER

PLACE IN CROCKERY-POT

COOK AT LOW, ALL DAY

41

HAM/LIMA BEANS

```
2 C   DRIED LIMA BEANS; SOAKED OVERNIGHT
         TO SOFTEN,   DRAINED              PLACE IN CROCKERY-POT
4 HAM HOCKS, OR 1 1/2 C  HAM PIECES
1  ONION, SLICED                           COOK AT LOW, ALL DAY
1/2  BELL PEPPER, DICED
1 (16-OUNCE) CAN STEWED TOMATOES
1 CAN   TOMATO SAUCE
1/4 C   MAPLE SYRUP
1  BAY LEAF
1 T  VINEGAR
1 TSP   DRY MUSTARD
1 T  SALT
1/2 TSP PEPPER
1/4 TSP GROUND CLOVES
```

HAM/PORK LOAF

```
1 1/2 LBS   PRECOOKED HAM, GROUND COARSLY
1 1/2 LBS   FRESH PORK, GROUND COARSLY     MIX AND FORM INTO LOAF
1  ONION, MINCED
1 C   BREAD CRUMBS                         PLACE IN CROCKERY-POT
1/2 C  SUGAR, FIRMLY PACKED
1/4 C  VINEGAR                             COOK ALL DAY, AT LOW
1 T  PREPARED MUSTARD
2 EGGS
1 C  MILK
```

HAM/SPICED

```
2-3 POUND   SMOKED BONELESS SHOULDER ROLL  PLACE IN CROCKERY-POT;
3 LEEKS, WHITE PART, SLICED                COOK ALL DAY, AT LOW
3 CARROTS, SLICED
1 STALK CELERY, SLICED                     DRAIN THROUGH COLANDER
1 POTATO, PEELED AND SLICED                INTO LARGE SAUCEPAN,
4 WHOLE CLOVES                             LEAVING MEAT AND
6 PEPPERCORNS                              VEGETABLES IN CROCKERY-
1/2 TSP  ALLSPICE                          POT
1 BAY LEAF, ON TOP FOR EASY REMOVAL
2 C  WATER

1 SMALL CABBAGE, IN WEDGES    COOKED IN LIQUID FROM CROCKERY-POT
```

42

JAM/FRUIT BUTTER

4 LBS APPLES,
   PEELED, QUARTERED
2 C APPLE CIDER
	OR PEACHES OR APRICOTS,
	     PEELED, PITTED
	CANNED FRUIT JUICE
		OR	4 (30-OUNCE)
			   CANS PEACHES
			   OR APRICOTS,
			   DRAINED

AND 1 C BROWN SUGAR, FIRMLY PACKED
3 C GRANULATED SUGAR
CINNAMON TO TASTE
GROUND CLOVES
ALLSPICE (WITH APPLES)
NUTMEG   (WITH APPLES)

PLACE IN CROCKERY-
POT WITH LID ON A
LITTLE CROOKED, SO
EXCESS MOISTURE CAN
ESCAPE; COOK AT
LOW, ALL DAY

LAMB/APPLES, ONIONS

3 LBS   LEAN LAMB STEW MEAT
FLOUR
SALT
PEPPER
OIL

DREDGE IN
FLOUR, AND
BROWN IN
OIL

PLACE IN CROCKERY-
POT

COOK AT LOW, ALL
DAY

4-5 TART APPLES, CORED, QUARTERED
12-18 WHOLE BOILING ONIONS, PEELED
1/2 C   BEEF BROTH (BOULLION)

LAMB/LEMON

3 LBS   LEAN LAMB, CUBED
OIL

BROWN IN
OIL, DRAIN

PLACE IN CROCKERY-POT

COOK AT LOW, ALL DAY

2 ONIONS, CHOPPED
1 CARROT, DICED
2 CLOVES GARLIC, MASHED
1 TSP SALT
1/4 TSP PEPPER
1 TSP OREGANO
1 (6-OUNCE) CAN V-8 VEGETABLE JUICE
1/2 C DRY WHITE WINE
1 LEMON, SLICED

LIQUID MAY BE
THICKENED WITH
CORNSTARCH

SERVE WITH NOODLES OR
RICE

LAMB/LOAF

3 LBS   LAMB, GROUND
1 ONION, MINCED
SALT
PEPPER
1/4 C   PINE NUTS
1/2 CUBE MARGARINE
1 C   CRACKED WHEAT SOAKED 10 MINUTES IN
      ICE WATER, AND SQUEEZED DRY

COMBINE INTO A LOAF

PLACE IN CROCKERY-POT

COOK AT LOW, ALL DAY

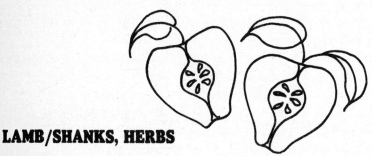

LAMB/SHANKS, HERBS

6 LAMB SHANKS, CUT IN HALF BY BUTCHER
1   ONION, SLICED
2   CLOVES GARLIC, MASHED
1/4 TSP   MARJORAM
1/4 TSP   THYME
1/4 TSP   ROSEMARY
1   T   WORCESTERSHIRE SAUCE
1 TSP   GARLIC SALT
1/4 TSP   PEPPER
1   C   WATER

PLACE IN CROCKERY-POT

COOK AT LOW, ALL DAY

LAMB/STEW

3 LBS   LAMB, CUBED
OIL

BROWN IN
OIL, DRAIN

2 TSP   SUGAR
1 1/2 TSP   SALT
1/4   TSP   PEPPER
2 TOMATOES, CHOPPED
2 CLOVES GARLIC, MASHED
3-4 CARROTS, IN CHUNKS
12-18 WHOLE BOILING ONIONS, PEELED
1 BAY LEAF, ON TOP FOR EASY REMOVAL
2 CANS   CHICKEN BROTH

PLACE IN CROCKERY-POT

COOK AT LOW, ALL DAY

LIQUID MAY BE THICKENED
WITH 2 T CORNSTARCH MIXED
WITH COLD WATER, TO AVOID
LUMPS

1 PKG   FROZEN PEAS
1 PKG   FROZEN GREEN BEANS

ADD TO CROCKERY-POT; CONTINUE
COOKING 30 MINUTES TO BLEND

LAMB/WINE

6 LAMB SHANKS, CUT IN HALF BY BUTCHER 1/2 CUBE MARGARINE OIL	BROWN, DRAIN	PLACE IN CROCKERY-POT COOK AT LOW, ALL DAY
2 ONIONS, CHOPPED 1 TSP PAPRIKA 1 TSP GROUND GINGER 1 TSP SALT 1/2 TSP FRESH GROUND PEPPER 1/2 C DRY WHITE WINE 1/2 C TOMATO JUICE 1 C CHICKEN BROTH		LIQUID MAY BE THICKENED WITH CORNSTARCH MIXED WITH COLD WATER TO AVOID LUMPS SERVE WITH FLUFFY WHITE RICE OR PILAF

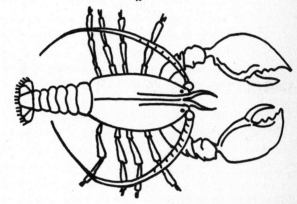

LOBSTER/NEWBURG

2 C FRESH OR FROZEN LOBSTER (CRAB, OR SHRIMP) 1 CAN FROZEN CREAM OF SHRIMP SOUP 1 C HALF-AND-HALF 1 T ONION, MINCED 1 TSP DRIED PARSLEY SALT, PEPPER 1/4 TSP PAPRIKA DASH CAYENNE DASH NUTMEG	PLACE IN CROCKERY-POT COOK ON LOW, 2 TO 3 HOURS; DO NOT OVERCOOK, BECAUSE FISH WILL BECOME MUSHY
2 EGG YOLKS 1/4 C SHERRY	BLEND INTO CROCKERY-POT, CONTINUE COOKING TO THICKEN
1/4 LB FRESH MUSHROOMS, SLICED BUTTER	SAUTE, ADD TO CROCKERY-POT SERVE IN INDIVIDUAL BAKED PIE SHELLS, OR OVER RICE

45

MEAT BALLS/ITALIAN

2 LBS   LEAN GROUND BEEF
1 LB   HOT BULK SAUSAGE, BROWNED, DRAINED
1/4 C   PACKAGED STUFFING MIX
1/2 TSP   GARLIC JUICE
1 T   DRIED PARSLEY
1 TSP   BASIL
SALT, PEPPER
2 EGGS
1/2 C   CONDENSED (CANNED) MILK

FLOUR
OLIVE OIL

MIX MEAT AND
SEASONINGS, FORM INTO
MEATBALLS

DREDGE IN FLOUR,
BROWN IN OLIVE OIL

PLACE IN
CROCKERY-POT

1 ONION, MINCED
5 CLOVES GARLIC, MASHED
2 T   DRIED PARSLEY
1 TSP   OREGANO
1 TSP   BASIL
5 LARGE DRIED MUSHROOMS, SOAKED TO
   SOFTEN; DRAINED, CHOPPED
SALT, PEPPER
1 CAN   BEEF BROTH (BOULLION)
1 LARGE CAN ITALIAN TOMATOES
2 CANS   TOMATO PASTE

MIX TOGETHER IN A BOWL,
POUR OVER MEATBALLS IN
CROCKERY-POT (THIS WILL
AVOID BREAKING-UP THE
BALLS)

COOK AT LOW, 4-6 HOURS;
OVER-COOKING WILL CAUSE
MEATBALLS TO BREAK APART

SPAGHETTI, COOKED
BUTTER, OR MARGARINE
CONDENSED GARLIC BREAD SPREAD
   OR   GARLIC OIL

MIX

SERVE MEATBALLS AND
SAUCE OVER GARLIC-
FLAVORED SPAGHETTI,
SPRINKLED WITH
PARMESAN CHEESE

MEAT BALLS/SWEDISH

1 LB   LEAN GROUND BEEF
1/4 LB   GROUND PORK
1 C   DRY BREAD CRUMBS
1/2 C   HALF-AND-HALF
2 EGGS
1 ONION, MINCED
SALT, PEPPER
1/2 TSP   DILL WEED
1/4 TSP   ALLSPICE
1/8 TSP   NUTMEG
1/8 TSP   CARDAMOM

FLOUR, OIL

MIX MEAT AND SEASONINGS, FORM
INTO MEATBALLS

DREDGE IN FLOUR, BROWN IN OIL

PLACE IN CROCKERY-POT

1 CAN BEEF BROTH (BOULLION)
1 C   HALF-AND-HALF
1/4 TSP   DILL WEED

ADD TO CROCKERY-POT
COOK AT LOW, 4-6 HOURS

THICKEN WITH CORNSTARCH DISSOLVED
IN COLD WATER TO AVOID LUMPS

MEATLOAF

3 LBS LEAN GROUND BEEF	
1/2 LB SAUSAGE, BROWNED, DRAINED	MIX AND FORM INTO LOAF
2 ENVL ONION SOUP MIX	
OR BEEF/MUSHROOM SOUP MIX	PLACE IN CROCKERY-POT
1 SMALL CAN EVAPORATED MILK	WITH POTATOES AROUND TOP
1 EGG	
1 ONION, CHOPPED	DO NOT ADD LIQUID
SMALL WHOLE BAKING POTATOES	COOK AT LOW, ALL DAY

MEATLOAF/ITALIAN

2 LBS LEAN GROUND BEEF	FORM INTO MEATLOAF
1 LB HOT BULK SAUSAGE, BROWNED, DRAINED	
1 C DRY BREAD CRUMBS	PLACE IN CROCKERY-POT
1 ONION, CHOPPED	
1 T DRIED PARSLEY	COOK AT LOW, ALL DAY
1 TSP OREGANO	
1/4 TSP BASIL	SLICE, AND LAY EACH
SALT, PEPPER	SLICE FLAT IN LARGE
1 EGG	BROILING PAN

MOZZARELLA CHEESE, SLICED	PLACE ON EACH MEATLOAF SLICE IN THE
TOMATOES, THICK SLICED	ORDER LISTED
GARLIC SALT, PEPPER	
OREGANO, DRIED PARSLEY	BROIL UNTIL MOZZARELLA MELTS, AND
PARMESAN CHEESE	PARMESAN CHEESE TURNS GOLDEN

MEATLOAF/MUSHROOM

1/2 C DRIED MUSHROOMS, SOAKED TO	
SOFTEN; DRAINED, MINCED	MIX AND FORM INTO LOAF
1 1/2 LBS LEAN GROUND BEEF	
1 ONION, MINCED	PLACE IN CROCKERY-POT
1 1/2 C COOKED RICE	
1 EGG	COOK AT LOW, ALL DAY
1/2 C MILK	
SALT, PEPPER	
1 TSP POWDERED GINGER	
1/2 TSP GARLIC POWDER	

47

MEATLOAF/OLIVES

2 LBS   LEAN GROUND BEEF
1   ONION, MINCED
2   STALKS CELERY, DICED
1 1/2 C   COOKED RICE
1   EGG
2   T   PREPARED MUSTARD
1/3 C   STUFFED OLIVES, SLICED
SALT, PEPPER
1/2 C   MILK
1 T   PREPARED MUSTARD

MIX AND FORM INTO LOAF

PLACE IN CROCKERY-POT

DO NOT ADD LIQUIDS

COOK AT LOW, ALL DAY

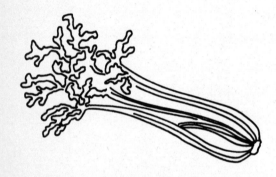

MEAT SAUCE   — SPAGHETTI

2-4 CANS MUSHROOMS
1 (16-OUNCE) CAN   STEWED TOMATOES
1 (15-OUNCE) CAN TOMATO SAUCE WITH TOMATO BITS
1 CAN   TOMATO SAUCE
1/4 C   WATER
1 CAN   TOMATO PASTE
2 ENVL   SPAGHETTI SAUCE MIX WITH MUSHROOMS
2   ONIONS, CHOPPED
2-4 CLOVES GARLIC, MASHED
1 LB   GROUND BEEF, BROWNED, DRAINED
1 LB   HOT BULK SAUSAGE, BROWNED, DRAINED
PEPPER
GARLIC SALT, TO TASTE
SALT, TO TASTE
OREGANO, TO TASTE

MIX IN
CROCKERY-POT

COOK AT LOW,
ALL DAY

CONTINUALLY
CHECK AND
CORRECT
SEASONINGS

SEVERAL HOT ITALIAN SAUSAGES, CUT IN 1/2-INCH
   CHUNKS, AND BROILED TO COOK AND MELT-OUT
   ALL FAT

ADD TO SAUCE
JUST BEFORE
SERVING

SPAGHETTI, COOKED
PARMESAN CHEESE

SERVE AS SAUCE OVER SPAGHETTI GARNISHED
WITH PARMESAN CHEESE; OR USE WHEN MAKING
LASAGNA, ETC.

48

MEAT STEW, MIXED

2 LBS BONELESS CHUCK ROAST, FAT REMOVED 1 LB BONELESS PORK ROAST, FAT REMOVED 3-4 PIECES CHICKEN 2 ONIONS, QUARTERED 3 CLOVES GARLIC, MASHED 3-4 CARROTS, IN CHUNKS 2 STALKS CELERY, SLICED SALT, PEPPER 1/2 TSP THYME 1/2 LB POLISH SAUSAGE, CUT-UP AND BROILED TO REMOVE FAT 1 BAY LEAF, ON TOP FOR EASY REMOVAL 1 CAN BEEF BROTH (BOULLION)	PLACE IN CROCKERY-POT WITH SAUSAGE AND BAY LEAF ON TOP COOK AT LOW, ALL DAY

OXTAILS/OLIVES

Ingredients	Prep	Instructions
4 LBS OXTAILS FLOUR SALT, PEPPER OIL	DREDGE IN FLOUR, BROWN IN OIL	PLACE IN CROCKERY-POT; COOK AT LOW, ALL DAY DRAIN THROUGH COLANDER INTO LARGE SAUCEPAN, LEAVING MEAT IN CROCKERY-POT
1 TSP CHILI POWDER 2 TSP DRY MUSTARD 1 (20-OUNCE) CAN PINEAPPLE JUICE 1 T LEMON JUICE WORCESTERSHIRE SAUCE SOY SAUCE		ADD ICE CUBES TO LIQUID IN SAUCEPAN; SKIM OFF ALL FAT WHICH WILL RISE TO THE TOP
DEFATTED LIQUID FROM CROCKERY-POT 1/2 C RAISINS 1 CAN PITTED BLACK OLIVES 1 BELL PEPPER, CHOPPED 3 STALKS CELERY, SLICED SALT, PEPPER		ADD TO DRAINED OXTAILS IN CROCKERY-POT, CONTINUE COOKING 30-60 MINUTES

OXTAILS/PEAS

4 LBS OXTAILS 1 ONION, CHOPPED SEASONED SALT PEPPER 1 CAN BEEF BROTH (BOULLION) BURGUNDY WINE	PLACE IN CROCKERY-POT; COOK AT LOW, ALL DAY DRAIN THROUGH COLANDER INTO LARGE SAUCEPAN, LEAVING MEAT IN POT ADD ICE CUBES TO LIQUID IN SAUCEPAN; SKIM OFF ALL FAT WHICH WILL RISE TO THE TOP
LIQUID FROM CROCKERY-POT 1 PKG WIDE EGG NOODLES 1 PKG FROZEN PEAS WATER, AS NEEDED	COOK IN SAUCEPAN UNTIL NOODLES DONE; ADD WATER AS NEEDED IF LIQUID IS ABSORBED PUT IN BUTTERED BAKING PAN
1 ONION, CHOPPED OXTAILS FROM CROCKERY-POT	SPRINKLE ONIONS OVER NOODLES, ADD OXTAILS COOK IN 400-DEGREE OVEN 10-15 MINUTES TO BLEND FLAVORS

OXTAILS/VEGETABLES

4 LBS OXTAILS, BROILED TO REMOVE FAT 1 ONION, MINCED 2 BEEF BOUILLION CUBES SALT, PEPPER 1 TSP GARLIC SALT 1 TSP SUGAR 1 BAY LEAF 6 WHOLE CLOVES 1 CAN BEEF BROTH (BOULLION) 1 CAN TOMATO SAUCE 1/4 C BURGUNDY WINE	PLACE IN CROCKERY-POT; COOK AT LOW, ALL DAY DRAIN THROUGH COLANDER INTO LARGE SAUCEPAN, LEAVING MEAT IN POT ADD ICE CUBES TO LIQUID IN SAUCEPAN; SKIM OFF ALL FAT WHICH WILL RISE TO THE TOP
LIQUID FROM CROCKERY-POT 1 LB CARROTS, IN CHUNKS 6 ONIONS, QUARTERED 2 SMALL ACORN SQUASHES, SLICED	COOK IN SAUCEPAN UNTIL DONE MIX WITH OXTAILS JUST BEFORE SERVING

1/2 CUBE BUTTER, NOT MARGARINE 1 C BOTTLED CLAM JUICE 1 QUART HALF-AND-HALF 1/4 TSP PAPRIKA SALT, PEPPER CAYENNE CELERY SALT WORCESTERSHIRE SAUCE	MIX IN CROCKERY-POT COOK AT LOW 1-2 HOURS
18-20 FRESH OYSTERS AND JUICE	ADD TO CROCKERY-POT COOK AT HIGH UNTIL EDGES OF OYSTERS CURL

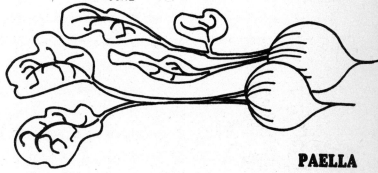

PAELLA

1-2 ONIONS, CHOPPED 2-3 CLOVES GARLIC, MASHED 1 BELL PEPPER, DICED 2 LARGE TOMATOES, DICED 1 (4-OUNCE) CAN PIMENTOS, DICED 2 CANS CHICKEN BROTH 2 TSP SALT 1/2 TSP PEPPER 2 T DRIED PARSLEY 1 TSP SAFFRON	PLACE IN CROCKERY-POT; BROWNED CHICKEN AND PORK ON TOP COOK 4-6 HOURS, AT LOW
3 LBS CHICKEN PARTS 1 LB PORK ROAST, IN STRIPS OLIVE OIL	BROWN IN OIL
1 LB FRESH OR FROZEN SHRIMP, COOKED 8-10 FRESH CLAMS, STEAM-COOKED; OR 1 (8-OUNCE) CAN 1 LB LOBSTER, COOKED, CUBED 1/2 LB GARLIC SAUSAGE, SLICED, BROILED 8 MUSSELS, COOKED 1 PKG FROZEN PEAS 4 C COOKED LONG GRAIN WHITE RICE	COMBINE IN VERY LARGE SAUCEPAN; ADD MIXTURE FROM CROCKERY-POT SIMMER 30 MINUTES TO BLEND FLAVORS

51

PASTRAMI

4 POUND CORNED BEEF BRISKET	PLACE IN CROCKERY-POT
2 ONIONS, SLICED	
2 CLOVES GARLIC, MASHED	COOK AT LOW, ALL DAY
1 T WHOLE BLACK PEPPERS	
1 T CORIANDER SEEDS	DRAIN, ALLOW MEAT TO COOL
8-10 WHOLE CLOVES	ENOUGH TO TOUCH
1 1/2 C WATER	

PEPPER	RUB THOROUGHLY INTO DRAINED MEAT
LIQUID SMOKE	
PAPRIKA	BAKE IN 350-DEGREE OVEN FOR 45 MINUTES

SLICE PAPER-THIN TO SERVE WITH RYE BREAD, MUSTARD, AND GARLIC DILL PICKLES

PORK/APPLES

3 POUND PORK ROAST, ALL VISIBLE FAT REMOVED, BROILED TO MELT-OUT HIDDEN FAT	PLACE IN CROCKERY-POT IN ORDER LISTED, WITH
1 ONION, CHOPPED	SUGAR-FILLED
CARROTS, IN CHUNKS	APPLES CAREFULLY
1 CLOVE GARLIC, CRUSHED	PLACED UPRIGHT
1 TSP DRIED ROSEMARY	
1 T FRESH GINGER, GRATED	
1 1/2 TSP SALT	COOK AT LOW,
1/2 TSP PEPPER	ALL DAY
YAMS OR SWEET POTATOES, SMALL, WHOLE	
NEW POTATOES, SMALL WHOLE	
SMALL GREEN APPLES, CORED HALF-WAY	
BROWN SUGAR PACKED INTO APPLES	
BRANDY SPRINKLED OVER SUGAR-PACKED APPLES	
2-3 BAY LEAVES, ON TOP FOR EASY REMOVAL	

PORK/BELL PEPPERS

Ingredients	Preparation	Instructions
3 LBS PORK, CUT INTO STRIPS	COAT PORK WITH SEASONINGS; PUT IN REFRIGERATOR 4 HOURS, OR OVERNIGHT	PLACE IN CROCKERY-POT
2 T CRUSHED GARLIC		
1 1/2 TSP SALT		COOK AT LOW, ALL DAY
1 TSP PEPPER		
OIL	BROWN MARINATED PORK, DRAIN	THICKEN LIQUID WITH CORNSTARCH DISSOLVED IN COLD WATER, TO AVOID LUMPS
2 BELL PEPPERS, SLICED		
2 RED BELL PEPPERS, SLICED		
OR 2 (4-OUNCE) CANS PIMENTOS, CHOPPED		
1-2 PURPLE ONIONS, QUARTERED		SERVE WITH RICE
1/2 C DRY WHITE WINE		
2 CHICKEN BOULLION CUBES		

PORK/CHOPS, GRAVY

6-8 THICK PORK CHOPS, DREDGE   PLACE IN CROCKERY-POT
    FAT REMOVED   IN FLOUR,
FLOUR   BROWN IN   COOK AT LOW, ALL DAY
SALT, PEPPER   OIL
OIL   SERVE WITH RICE OR
                                MASHED POTATOES

2 CLOVES GARLIC, MASHED
1 CAN MUSHROOMS, DRAINED
1 CAN TOMATO PASTE
1 CAN   CREAM OF MUSHROOM SOUP
GARLIC SALT
PEPPER

PORK/FRUIT

6-8 THICK PORK CHOPS, BROWN,
    FAT REMOVED   DRAIN   PLACE IN CROCKERY-POT
BUTTER AND OIL
                            COOK AT LOW, ALL DAY
6-8 TART APPLES, UNPEELED, SLICED
1/2 C   DRIED CURRANTS
1/2 C   DRIED APRICOTS
1   C   WALNUTS, CHOPPED
1/2 TSP   CINNAMON
1/2 C   HONEY
1/4 C   WATER
2   T   BRANDY

PORK/ORANGE

6-8 THICK PORK CHOPS, BROWN,
    FAT REMOVED   DRAIN   PLACE IN CROCKERY-POT
OIL
                            COOK AT LOW, ALL DAY
1   ONION, CHOPPED
1   STALK CELERY, CHOPPED   GARNISH WITH VERY
SALT, PEPPER   THIN SLICES OF FRESH
PINCH THYME   ORANGE
1/2 C   ORANGE JUICE
1 ORANGE, PEELED, SLICED (NOTE:
   WHITE MEMBRANE BECOMES BITTER)
2 T   WINE VINEGAR

53

PORK/PIG'S FEET

NOTE: PIGS FEET DO NOT APPEAL TO EVERYONE,
      BE CAUTIOUS IF SERVING GUESTS

PIGS FEET, SPLIT BY BUTCHER   PLACE IN CROCKERY-POT
WATER TO COVER
                                     COOK AT LOW, ALL DAY

            PUT IN SAUCEPAN IN REFRIGERATOR, FAT WILL RISE
            TO THE TOP AND HARDEN

            REMOVE FAT LAYER; HEAT TO LIQUIFY GELATIN,
            REMOVE PIGS FEET AND PUT IN GLASS BOWL

TO PICKLE: USE PROPORTION OF
       1 C DEFATTED, LIQUIFIED GELATIN   COVER PIGS FEET WITH
            FROM COOKING PIGS FEET   MARINADE AND PUT IN
       1/4 C VINEGAR   REFRIGERATOR FOR
       2 T SUGAR   24 HOURS, OR LONGER
       5-6 CLOVES
       ONION, THINLY SLICED   SERVE HOT, OR COLD

PORK/POT-ROASTED

5-6 POUND PORK ROAST; ALL VISIBLE FAT REMOVED,
            AND BROILED 30 MINUTES TO   PLACE IN
            MELT-OUT HIDDEN FAT   CROCKERY-POT
1-2 CLOVES GARLIC, SLICED; INSERTED IN SLITS
            CUT IN DEFATTED ROAST   COOK AT LOW,
2-3 ONIONS, SLICED   ALL DAY
SOY SAUCE , RUBBED INTO MEAT
GARLIC SALT
PEPPER
1/2 C WATER

PORK/RIBS, HONEY

4-5 LBS SPARERIBS, SPLIT IN HALF BY BUTCHER;
            BROILED TO MELT-OUT HIDDEN FAT   PLACE IN
                                                CROCKERY-POT
CARROTS, IN CHUNKS
1 ONION, MINCED   COOK AT LOW,
1 T LEMON JUICE, OR VINEGAR   ALL DAY
1 T SOY SAUCE
1 T CURRY POWDER
SALT, PEPPER
1/2 C HONEY

54

PORK/RIBS, SAUERKRAUT

4 LBS SPARERIBS, SPLIT IN HALF BY BUTCHER;
        BROILED TO MELT-OUT HIDDEN FAT
1 (27-OUNCE) CAN SAUERKRAUT, DRAINED
1/2 LB TART APPLES, SLICED THINLY
1 ONION, MINCED
1 CLOVE GARLIC, MASHED
2 T   CARAWAY SEEDS
10 CLOVES
1 TSP SALT
1/4 TSP PEPPER
1 BAY LEAF, ON TOP FOR EASY REMOVAL
1 C DRY WHITE WINE

PLACE IN CROCKERY-POT

COOK AT LOW, ALL DAY

PORK/ROAST, MADEIRA SAUCE

4-5 POUND PORK ROAST; ALL VISIBLE FAT REMOVED,
            AND BROILED 30 MINUTES TO
            MELT-OUT HIDDEN FAT
4-5 BAY LEAVES, SPLIT; INSERTED IN DEEP SLITS
            CUT IN DEFATTED ROAST

PLACE IN CROCKERY-POT

COOK AT LOW, ALL DAY

DRAIN THROUGH COLANDER INTO SAUCE-PAN; REMOVE BAY LEAVES FROM ROAST

LIQUID FROM CROCKERY-POT, FAT SKIIMED OFF
1/4 C FLOUR, DISSOLVED IN COLD WATER
SALT, PEPPER
1/2 C MADEIRA WINE

COOK IN SAUCEPAN UNTIL THICKENED

SERVE OVER SLICED MEAT

PORK/ROAST, PINEAPPLE

5 POUND PORK ROAST, ALL VISIBLE FAT REMOVED,
            AND BROILED TO REMOVE HIDDEN FAT
1 ONION, SLICED
1 BELL PEPPER, CHOPPED
1/4 C BROWN SUGAR, FIRMLY PACKED
1 CAN CRUSHED PINEAPPLE
1 T TOMATO PASTE
2 T SOY SAUCE
SALT, PEPPER

PLACE IN CROCKERY-POT

COOK AT LOW, ALL DAY

FRESH PINEAPPLE SPEARS   SERVE WITH SLICED PORK ROAST

PORK/ROAST, SAUSAGE

4-6 POUND BONED PORK ROAST, ALL VISIBLE FAT REMOVED, BROILED TO MELT-OUT HIDDEN FAT		SEAL STUFFED PORK TIGHTLY IN FOIL
PARTIALLY SLICED THROUGH INTO THICK LAYERS FOR INSERTING STUFFING MIX		
		PLACE IN CROCKERY-POT
1/2 LB HOT BULK SAUSAGE, BROWNED, DRAINED	MIX,	
1 (6-1/2 OUNCE) BAG CORNBREAD STUFFING MIX	STUFF	
1 APPLE, CHOPPED	BETWEEN	COOK AT
1 ONION, MINCED	EACH	LOW, ALL
2 STALKS CELERY, DICED	LAYER	DAY
1 T SOY SAUCE	OF PORK	
1 EGG	ROAST	
SALT, PEPPER		
1 TSP THYME		
1 TSP SAGE		
1 TSP BASIL		

PORK/SAUERKRAUT GOULASH

2-3 LBS PORK, IN CUBES	BROWN	
OIL	DRAIN	PLACE IN CROCKERY-POT
3 ONIONS, CHOPPED		COOK AT LOW, ALL DAY
2 T PAPRIKA		
1 T CARAWAY SEEDS		TURN-OFF A FEW MINUTES
1 (27-OUNCE) CAN SAUERKRAUT, DRAINED		BEFORE READY TO SERVE
1 C SOUR CREAM		STIR INTO COOLED CROCKERY-POT MIXTURE

PORK/SAUSAGE, SAUERKRAUT

1 (27-OUNCE) CAN SAUERKRAUT, DRAINED	PLACE IN CROCKERY-POT
1 ONION, CHOPPED	
1 CAN STEWED TOMATOES	COOK AT LOW, SEVERAL
1/2 TSP CARAWAY SEED	HOURS TO ALL DAY
1 T BROWN SUGAR	
1 STRIP BACON, UNCOOKED, MINCED	
1 LB ITALIAN SAUSAGE	CUT INTO CHUNKS AND BROIL UNTIL DONE,
1 LB POLISH SAUSAGE	AND MOST OF FAT MELTS-OUT
	MIX INTO CROCKERY-POT AND HEAT TO BLEND
	SERVE WITH POTATO PANCAKES

56

PORK/STEW

2-3 LBS PORK, IN CHUNKS, BROWNED IN SKILLET
      TO MELT-OUT FAT
2 ONIONS, DICED
1 BELL PEPPER, DICED ‖ BROWNED IN OIL,
1 C RAW RICE   DRAINED
2-3 POTATOES, DICED
OLIVE OIL

3 TOMATOES, DICED
SALT, PEPPER
3 TSP PAPRIKA
1/2 CAN BEEF BROTH (BOULLION)

PLACE IN
CROCKERY-POT

COOK AT LOW,
ALL DAY

PORK/SWEET POTATO

3 LBS PORK, IN CHUNKS, BROILED TO MELT-OUT
      HIDDEN FAT
1 STALK CELERY, SLICED
1 T DRIED PARSLEY
SALT, PEPPER
3 APPLES, PEELED, SLICED
1 BAY LEAF
1 ONION, CHOPPED
1/2 CAN BEEF BROTH (BOULLION)
2-3 YAMS, OR SWEET POTATOES, PEELED, SLICED

PLACE IN
CROCKERY-POT

COOK AT LOW,
ALL DAY

PORK/SWEET & SOUR

4 LBS   PORK, IN CHUNKS, BROILED TO MELT-OUT
      HIDDEN FAT
SALT, PEPPER
1 BELL PEPPER, SLICED
8-12 WHOLE BOILING ONIONS, PEELED
1 CAN PINEAPPLE CHUNKS, DRAINED
2 TOMATOES, CHOPPED
2 T VINEGAR
1/3 C BROWN SUGAR, FIRMLY PACKED
1/4 C SOY SAUCE
1/2 C CHICKEN BROTH
1/4 C CORNSTARCH DISSOLVED IN COLD WATER

PLACE IN
CROCKERY-POT

COOK AT LOW,
ALL DAY

57

POTATOES/BAKED

SMALL BAKING POTATOES, GREASED   PLACE IN CROCKERY-
      DO NOT CUT UNPEELED POTATOES BECAUSE   POT; COOK AT LOW,
      THE BROWN SKIN WILL DISCOLOR THE   ALL DAY, OR AT
      WHITE INSIDE   HIGH SEVERAL HOURS

DICED BACON, BROWNED, DRAINED
GREEN ONION, TOPS ONLY, CHOPPED   GARNISH BAKED POTATOES
BUTTER, NOT MARGARINE
SOUR CREAM
SALT, PEPPER

POTATOES/SCALLOPED

5-6 POTATOES, PEELED, SLICED   PLACE IN CROCKERY-POT
1 CAN   CREAM OF MUSHROOM SOUP
1/2 ONION, CHOPPED   COOK AT LOW, ALL DAY
SALT, PEPPER

1/2 LB FRESH MUSHROOMS, SLICED   SAUTE, ADD TO CROCKERY-POT
1/2 ONION, MINCED   JUST BEFORE SERVING
BUTTER

POTATOES, SWEET/APPLES

4 SWEET POTATOES, PEELED, QUARTERED
4 TART APPLES, PEELED, QUARTERED   PLACE IN CROCKERY-POT
1/4 C SUGAR
1/2 C DARK BROWN SUGAR, FIRMLY PACKED   COOK AT LOW, ALL DAY
1/4 TSP NUTMEG
1/2 TSP SALT
1/4 C   WATER

1/2 CUBE MARGARINE
1/2 C WALNUTS, CHOPPED   ADD TO MIXTURE IN CROCKERY-POT

POTATOES, SWEET/APRICOTS

4 SWEET POTATOES, PEELED, SLICED ‖ PLACE IN CROCKERY-
1 (16-OUNCE) CAN PITTED APRICOTS, DRAINED ‖ POT; COOK AT LOW,
1/2 C DARK BROWN SUGAR, FIRMLY PACKED ‖ ALL DAY
1/2 C ORANGE JUICE

DRAIN AND MASH

1/2 CUBE MARGARINE
1/2 C PECANS OR ALMONDS, SLIVERED ‖ ADD TO MASHED POTATOES

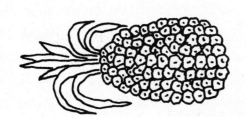

POTATOES, SWEET/PECANS

4 SWEET POTATOES, PEELED, SLICED ‖ PLACE IN CROCKERY-POT;
3/4 C BROWN SUGAR, FIRMLY PACKED ‖ COOK AT LOW, ALL DAY
1 TSP CINNAMON
1/4 TSP NUTMEG ‖ DRAIN AND MASH
1 TSP SALT
1/2 C ORANGE JUICE

1/2 CUBE MARGARINE
3/4 C PECANS, CHOPPED ‖ ADD TO MASHED POTATOES

POTATOES, SWEET/PINEAPPLE

4 SWEET POTATOES, PEELED, SLICED ‖ PLACE IN CROCKERY-POT:
1 CAN CRUSHED PINEAPPLE ‖ COOK AT LOW, ALL DAY
1/2 C BROWN SUGAR, FIRMLY PACKED

1/2 CUBE MARGARINE ‖ ADD TO MASHED POTATOES

PUDDING/CHERRY-TAPIOCA

2 C CANNED PITTED SOUR CHERRIES, DRAINED	MIX IN CROCKERY-POT
2 C LIQUID (CHERRY JUICE AND WATER)	
1/2 C QUICK-COOKING TAPIOCA	COOK AT LOW, SEVERAL
1 1/2 C SUGAR	HOURS
1/2 TSP SALT	
1/4 TSP NUTMEG	
1/2 TSP CINNAMON	
1/4 CUBE BUTTER OR MARGARINE	
1/2 TSP VANILLA	
RED FOOD COLORING	

PUDDING/CHOCOLATE

2 T CRISCO SHORTENING	POUR INTO GREASED AND FLOURED COFFEE
1/2 C SUGAR, MIXED WITH	CAN OR MOLD WHICH FITS LOOSELY INTO
SHORTENING	CROCKERY-POT -COVER TOP OF MOLD
1 EGG	TIGHTLY WITH FOIL
3/4 C MILK	
1 3/4 C FLOUR	POUR 1-2 C WATER BETWEEN MOLD AND
3 TSP BAKING POWDER	SIDE OF CROCKERY-POT; DO NOT FILL
1/4 TSP SALT	ABOVE 1/2-INCH FROM TOP OF MOLD
4 T COCOA	
1 TSP VANILLA	PUT LID ON CROCKERY-POT AND
1/2 C CHOPPED WALNUTS	COOK ON HIGH, 4-6 HOURS

PUDDING/DATE

1/4 C CRISCO SHORTENING		
1/4 CUBE MARGARINE	CREAMED	FOLLOW DIRECTIONS ABOVE
1/2 C SUGAR	TOGETHER	FOR CHOCOLATE PUDDING,
1/4 C DARK BROWN SUGAR,		OR COOK WITHOUT WATER
FIRMLY PACKED		FOR A CAKE-LIKE DATE
		PUDDING:
3 EGGS		
1 C MILK		COVER TOP OF MOLD WITH
1 1/2 C FLOUR		5 PAPER TOWELS, PUT
1 TSP SALT		LID ON CROCKERY-POT;
1 (8-OUNCE) PKG PITTED DATES, CHOPPED		COOK ON HIGH 4-6 HOURS
1/2 C WALNUTS, CHOPPED		
1/4 C RAISINS		
1/2 TSP CINNAMON		
1/8 TSP MACE		
3/4 TSP ALLSPICE		
1 T LEMON JUICE		
1 TSP VANILLA		

60

PUDDING/PERSIMMON

1 T MARGARINE, AT ROOM TEMPERATURE
1 C   SUGAR, BLENDED WITH MARGARINE
1 C + 1 T   FLOUR
1/4 C   DATE SUGAR (OPTIONAL)
1 TSP   BAKING SODA
1/2 TSP   SALT
1 TSP CINNAMON
1/2 TSP   NUTMEG
1 C PERSIMMON PULP   (UNRIPE
      PERSIMMON MAY BE RIPENED BY
      FREEZING THOROUGHLY, THAWING)
1/4 C   MILK
1 TSP   VANILLA
1 C   RAISINS AND CHOPPED DATES
1 C CHOPPED WALNUTS AND
         SLIVERED ALMONDS

FOLLOW DIRECTIONS
FOR CHOCOLATE PUDDING;
      OR, COOK WITHOUT
WATER FOR A
PERSIMMON CAKE:
   ADD 1/2 C   FLOUR
      1 1/2 TSP
         BAKING POWDER
      1/4 C   MILK

   COVER TOP OF MOLD
   WITH 5 PAPER TOWELS,
   PUT LID ON CROCKERY-
   POT; COOK ON HIGH
   4-6 HOURS

1 CUBE BUTTER, AT ROOM TEMPERATURE
1 1/2 C POWDERED SUGAR
1/2 C   HEAVY CREAM
1 TSP   ALMOND EXTRACT
1 TSP   VANILLA EXTRACT

BLEND TOGETHER AND SERVE
AS SAUCE WITH PUDDING OR
CAKE

PUDDING/PLUM

1 CUBE MARGARINE, AT ROOM TEMPERATURE
3/4 C   BROWN SUGAR, FIRMLY PACKED
3/4 C   FINE DRY BREAD CRUMBS
1/2 C   FLOUR
1/2 TSP   BAKING SODA
1/4 TSP   SALT
1 TSP   GROUND CINNAMON
1/2 TSP   GROUND CLOVES
3   EGGS
1 (30-OUNCE) CAN PURPLE PLUMS, DRAINED,
      PITTED, CHOPPED
1 (8-OUNCE) PKG   PITTED DATES, CHOPPED
1 C   RAISINS, MUSKAT OR SEEDLESS
1 C   PECANS,WALNUTS,OR ALMONDS; CHOPPED
1 (8-OUNCE) PKG CHOPPED CANDIED FRUITS

FOLLOW DIRECTIONS
FOR COOKING
CHOCOLATE PUDDING
ON PAGE 60

1 CUBE BUTTER, AT ROOM TEMPERATURE
1 1/2 C   POWDERED SUGAR
2 T, OR MORE, LIGHT RUM

BLEND AND SERVE OVER
PLUM PUDDING

61

PUDDING/PRUNE-TAPIOCA

1/2 LB PITTED PRUNES, CHOPPED	MIX IN CROCKERY-POT
1/2 C QUICK-COOKING TAPIOCA	
1/3 C SUGAR	COOK AT LOW, SEVERAL HOURS
1/2 TSP SALT	
1 T LEMON JUICE	
2 C WATER	

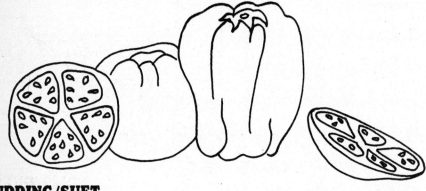

PUDDING/SUET

1 C SUET, CHOPPED FINE - AVAILABLE FROM YOUR BUTCHER	POUR INTO GREASED AND FLOURED COFFEE CAN OR MOLD
1 C BREAD CRUMBS	WHICH FITS LOOSELY INTO
2 C FLOUR	CROCKERY-POT - COVER TOP
1 TSP SODA	OF MOLD TIGHTLY WITH FOIL
1 TSP SALT	
1 TSP CINNAMON	POUR 1-2 C WATER BETWEEN
1/2 TSP GROUND CLOVES	MOLD AND SIDE OF POT;
1 C MILK	DO NOT FILL ABOVE 1/2-INCH
1 C MOLASSES	FROM TOP OF MOLD
1 C RAISINS	
	PUT LID ON CROCKERY-POT AND COOK ON HIGH, 4-6 HOURS
1/2 CUBE MARGARINE, AT ROOM TEMPERATURE	
1 1/2 C POWDERED SUGAR	
1 EGG WHITE, BEATEN	BLEND AND SERVE OVER
JUICE OF 1 LEMON	SUET PUDDING

RABBIT/ROASTED

1 OR 2 RABBITS, CUT-UP	DREDGE IN FLOUR; BROWN IN OIL
FLOUR	
SALT, PEPPER	PLACE IN CROCKERY-POT;
OIL	COOK AT LOW, ALL DAY

RICE/ALMONDS

2 C LONG GRAIN WHITE RICE 3 C CANNED BEEF BROTH (BOULLION) AND WATER SALT, PEPPER	PLACE IN CROCKERY-POT; COOK AT HIGH 1 1/4 HOURS, STIR OCCASIONALLY
1 SMALL CAN CRUSHED PINEAPPLE, WELL DRAINED 1/2 C SLICED ALMONDS	STIR INTO RICE BEFORE SERVING

GREEN ONION TOPS, SLICED FOR GARNISH

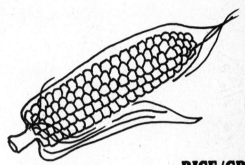

RICE/GREEN

2 C LONG GRAIN WHITE RICE 3 C CHICKEN BROTH AND WATER 4 T ONION FLAKES 4 T PARSLEY FLAKES 4 T BELL PEPPER FLAKES SALT, PEPPER 1/2 CUBE MARGARINE, OR BUTTER	PLACE IN CROCKERY-POT COOK AT HIGH 1 1/4 HOURS, STIRRING OCCASIONALLY
1 1/2 C ROMANO & PARMESAN CHEESE GREEN ONION TOPS, SLICED	SPRINKLE OVER RICE BEFORE SERVING

RICE/PILAF, BEEF

2 C LONG GRAIN WHITE RICE 3 C CANNED BEEF BROTH (BOULLION) AND WATER SALT PEPPER, MORE THAN YOU WOULD USUALLY USE	PLACE IN CROCKERY-POT; COOK AT HIGH, 1 1/4 HOURS, STIR OCCASIONALLY
1 LB DICED BACON, FRIED CRISP, DRAINED GREEN ONION TOPS, SLICED 3-4 (4-OUNCE) CANS SLICED MUSHROOMS 1/2 LARGE ONION, MINCED	MIX INTO RICE BEFORE SERVING

RICE/PILAF, CHICKEN

2 C LONG GRAIN WHITE RICE 2 1/2 C CHICKEN BROTH 1/2 C SHERRY WINE 1/2 CUBE MARGARINE 1 ONION, MINCED 1 CLOVE GARLIC, CRUSHED 1 T DRIED PARSLEY SALT, PEPPER	PLACE IN CROCKERY-POT COOK AT HIGH 1 1/4 HOURS; STIRRING OCCASIONALLY
1/4 C RAISINS (OPTIONAL) 1/4 C PINE NUTS (OPTIONAL)	MIX INTO RICE BEFORE SERVING

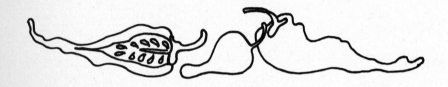

RICE/SPANISH

2 C LONG GRAIN WHITE RICE 3 T OLIVE OIL	BROWN IN OIL	PLACE IN CROCKERY-POT
1 1/2 C TOMATO SAUCE AND TOMATO JUICE 1 1/2 C BEEF BROTH (BOULLION) 1/2 CUBE MARGARINE 2 TOMATOES, CHOPPED 1 ONION, CHOPPED 1 BELL PEPPER, CHOPPED SALT, PEPPER GARLIC POWDER 1 T WORCESTERSHIRE SAUCE 1 T PIMENTO, CHOPPED		COOK AT HIGH 1 1/4 HOURS; STIRRING OCCASIONALLY
1 LB SAUSAGE LINKS, SLICED THINLY; FRIED TO COOK AND MELT-OUT FAT, DRAIN		MIX INTO RICE BEFORE SERVING

RICE/STEAMED

2 C LONG GRAIN WHITE RICE 3 C WATER 1/2 CUBE MARGARINE 1-2 CLOVES GARLIC, CRUSHED SALT, PEPPER	PLACE IN CROCKERY-POT COOK AT HIGH 1 1/4 HOURS; STIRRING OCCASIONALLY

```
2 C  RICE
1/2 CUBE MARGARINE   SAUTE UNTIL      PLACE IN CROCKERY-POT
1 ONION, MINCED      ONION LIMP
                                      COOK AT HIGH 1 1/4
2 1/4 C  CHICKEN BROTH                HOURS;  STIRRING
3/4 C  DRY WHITE WINE                 OCCASIONALLY
1 TSP SALT
1/8 TSP, OR MORE, SAFFRON


PARMESAN CHEESE   SPRINKLE OVER RICE BEFORE SERVING
```

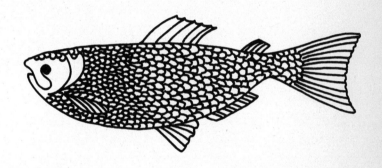

SALMON/LOAF

```
1 (16-OUNCE) CAN SALMON, UNDRAINED, FLAKED   PLACE IN CROCKERY-
2  EGGS                                      POT
1/2 C  MILK
1 C  SOFT BREAD CRUMBS                        COOK AT LOW, 5-7
1 T  LEMON JUICE                             HOURS
1 T  DRIED PARSLEY
3/4 TSP  CELERY SALT
1/2 TSP  GARLIC SALT
1/8 TSP  PEPPER


1 CAN  MUSHROOMS, SLICED       HEAT IN SAUCEPAN, SERVE AS
2 C  WHITE SAUCE               SAUCE OVER SALMON
1/4 C  AMERICAN CHEESE, GRATED
1 TSP, OR MORE, PAPRIKA
```

SHRIMP/CURRY

1 ONION, THINLY SLICED 1 CLOVE GARLIC, MINCED 1/2 CUBE MARGARINE	SAUTE	PLACE IN CROCKERY-POT COOK AT LOW, 3-5 HOURS

2   CHICKEN BOULLION CUBES
2 1/2 C HALF-AND-HALF
    OR 1 CAN FROZEN SHRIMP SOUP
        1 C HALF-AND-HALF
    OR 2 C CLAM JUICE
1/4 BAY LEAF, CRUMBLED
CURRY POWDER, TO TASTE
1/4 C FLOUR, DISSOLVED IN COLD WATER
SALT, PEPPER

2-3 LBS CLEANED FRESH OR FROZEN SHRIMP   SIMMER 3-5 MINUTES TO
1 T PICKLING SPICE   COOK; DRAIN, MIX INTO
1 QUART BOILING WATER, IN A SAUCEPAN   CROCKERY-POT

                                             SERVE OVER RICE

1 LB DICED BACON, FRIED CRISP, DRAINED   SERVE AS CONDIMENTS
1 ONION, CHOPPED   IN SMALL SERVING
BOILED EGGS, CHOPPED   DISHES
GREEN ONION TOPS, CHOPPED
ALMONDS, SLICED OR SLIVERED
RAISINS
CHUTNEY

SHRIMP/CURRY, INDIAN

2 ONIONS, MINCED 1 CLOVE GARLIC, MINCED 2 T PEANUT OIL	SAUTE	PLACE IN CROCKERY-POT COOK AT LOW, 3-5 HOURS

1/4 TSP GINGER
1 TSP SALT
1/2 TSP CHILI POWDER
1 1/2 TSP, OR MORE, CURRY POWDER
1/8 TSP TUMERIC
1 TSP VINEGAR
1 C TOMATOES, CHOPPED
1/2 C WATER

                                             SIMMER 3-5 MINUTES TO
2-3 LBS CLEANED FRESH OR FROZEN SHRIMP   COOK; DRAIN, ADD TO
BOILING WATER, IN A SAUCEPAN   CROCKERY-POT

66   SERVE OVER RICE

SHRIMP/RICE

1 1/2 C LONG GRAIN WHITE RICE   PLACE IN CROCKERY-POT
2 C CHICKEN BROTH
1 SMALL CAN EVAPORATED MILK   COOK AT HIGH, 1 1/4
1/2 C CATSUP   HOURS, STIRRING
1 T WORCESTERSHIRE SAUCE   OCCASIONALLY
1 T DRIED PARSLEY
SALT, PEPPER

1 LB FRESH MUSHROOMS, SLICED
BUTTER   SAUTE   MIX INTO CROCKERY-POT;
     CONTINUE COOKING TO
1 LB COOKED, CLEANED FRESH SHRIMP   BLEND FLAVORS
1/2 C AMERICAN CHEESE, GRATED

SOUP/BEAN, HAM

1 LB DRIED NAVY BEANS, SOAKED OVERNIGHT
     IN SEVERAL QUARTS OF WATER, DRAINED   PLACE IN CROCKERY-
2 HAM HOCKS   POT
1/2 LB DICED BACON, BROWNED, DRAINED
1 ONION, MINCED   COOK AT LOW, ALL
2 CLOVES GARLIC, MINCED   DAY
1 STALK CELERY, MINCED
2 T DRIED PARSLEY
SALT, PEPPER
1 C HALF-AND-HALF
4-6 C WATER

SOUP/BEAN, SALT PORK

1 LB DRIED WHITE BEANS, SOAKED OVERNIGHT
     IN SEVERAL QUARTS OF WATER, DRAINED   PLACE IN CROCKERY-
1/2 LB LEAN SALT PORK, PARBOILED FOR   POT
     20 MINUTES, DRAINED
1 LEEK, MINCED   COOK AT LOW, ALL
2 T DRIED PARSLEY   DAY
SALT, PEPPER

4 ONIONS, MINCED   SAUTE   ADD ONIONS AND
OIL   CELERY, CONTINUE
     BOILED IN SAUCEPAN   COOKING JUST TO
1 CELERY HEART   UNTIL TENDER, DICED   BLEND FLAVORS

THIN SLICED BREAD, TOASTED   SERVE BUTTERED TOAST FLOATING
BUTTER   ON BOWLS OF SOUP, HEAVILY
PARMESAN CHEESE   SPRINKLED WITH CHEESE

SOUP/BEEF, VEGETABLE

4 LBS CROSS-CUT BEEF SHANKS   PLACE IN CROCKERY-POT;
SMALL SOUP BONES WITH MARROW   COOK AT LOW, 8-12 HOURS
1 ONION, CHOPPED
CELERY, SLICED   REFRIGERATE FOR SEVERAL HOURS;
SALT, PEPPER   REMOVE LAYER OF FAT WHICH WILL
WATER TO COVER   RISE TO THE TOP

                                 REMOVE BONES, LEAVING MARROW;
                                 CHOP MEAT

COOKED MEAT AND BROTH
2 ONIONS, MINCED   PLACE IN
2 CARROTS, GRATED   CROCKERY-POT
2 STALKS CELERY, DICED
2 T DRIED PARSLEY   COOK AT LOW,
1/4 C SOY SAUCE   ALL DAY
1/4 C WORCESTERSHIRE SAUCE
GARLIC POWDER
4-6 BEEF BOULLION CUBES
1 CAN TOMATO PASTE
1 CAN STEWED TOMATOES
1/4 C FLOUR, DISSOLVED IN COLD WATER
WATER TO FILL CROCKERY-POT, 1/2-INCH FROM TOP
SALT, PEPPER

SOUP/BOUILLON, BEEF

1 LB BEEF STEW MEAT, CHOPPED
1/2 LB CHICKEN GIBLETS, CHOPPED   ROAST IN 450-DEGREE
1 CHICKEN CARCASS   OVEN, 30 MINUTES
1 LB MARROW BONES, CRACKED
1 VEAL KNUCKLE, CRACKED BY BUTCHER

1 CARROT, CHOPPED   ADD TO ROASTING MEAT AND BONES;
1 ONION, CHOPPED   COOK ANOTHER 30 MINUTES, TURN DOWN
1 STALK CELERY, CHOPPED   TO 350-DEGREES IF SCORCHING
FRESH PARSLEY, CHOPPED

BROWNED MEAT, BONES, VEGETABLES
1 ONION, CHOPPED   PLACE IN CROCKERY-
2 CLOVES   POT; COOK AT LOW,
1 CLOVE GARLIC, MASHED   ALL DAY
1 CARROT, SLICED
1 LEEK (WHITE PART) THINLY SLICED   STRAIN THROUGH
1 CELERY STALK, SLICED   COLANDER TO
2 T DRIED PARSLEY   REMOVE MEAT, BONES
1/2 TSP THYME   AND VEGETABLES
1 BAY LEAF
SALT, PEPPER   STRAIN THROUGH
WATER TO FILL CROCKERY-POT, 1/2-INCH FROM TOP   CHEESECLOTH

SOUP/BOUILLON, CHICKEN

1 4-5 LB STEWING HEN, CUT-UP GIBLETS, CHOPPED	ROAST IN 450-DEGREE OVEN, 30 MINUTES
BROWNED MEAT, DRAINED 1 CARROT, GRATED 1 LEEK (WHITE PART) THINLY SLICED 2 T DRIED PARSLEY 1/2 TSP THYME 1 BAYLEAF SALT, PEPPER WATER TO FILL CROCKERY-POT, 1/2-INCH FROM TOP	PLACE IN CROCKERY-POT; COOK AT LOW, ALL DAY REMOVE SCUM OCCASIONALLY (ADD ICE CUBES TO MAKE IT RISE) TO KEEP LIQUID CLEAR DRAIN THROUGH COLANDER TO REMOVE MEAT, BONES VEGETABLES STRAIN THROUGH CHEESECLOTH

SOUP/CHICKEN

CHICKEN CARCASS, OR FRESH NECKS, BACKS, WINGS 1/2 ONION, MINCED 1 STALK CELERY, DICED 2 CHICKEN BOULLION CUBES 6 PEPPERCORNS 4 WHOLE CLOVES DASH NUTMEG DASH MACE 1 BAY LEAF WATER TO COVER	PLACE IN CROCKERY-POT; COOK AT LOW, ALL DAY STRAIN; RETURN BROTH TO CROCKERY-POT
1 C, OR MORE, COOKED CHICKEN; BONES AND SKIN REMOVED 1/2 ONION, MINCED 1/4 C FLOUR, DISSOLVED IN COLD WATER SALT, PEPPER NOODLES	ADD TO BROTH IN CROCKERY-POT; TURN TO HIGH TO COOK NOODLES AND BLEND FLAVORS

NOTE: FOR CREAM-OF-CHICKEN SOUP,
       USE 1 C CREAM FOR EACH
       CUP OF CHICKEN BROTH

SOUP/CLAM CHOWDER, RED

FOLLOW RECIPE BELOW FOR WHITE CLAM CHOWDER,
BUT SUBSTITUTE:
         1 (30-OUNCE) CAN TOMATOES, UNDRAINED
               FOR 2 C MILK
AND ADD 2 CARROTS, GRATED
         2 STALKS CELERY, MINCED
         1 BELL PEPPER, MINCED
         1 T DRIED PARSLEY
         1 TSP DRIED THYME
         1 BAY LEAF
         3 WHOLE CLOVES
         1 CARDAMON
         1/4 TSP COARSE GROUND PEPPER

SOUP/CLAM CHOWDER, WHITE

18-25 FRESH CLAMS, IN SHELLS   STEAM UNTIL TENDER; DRAIN,
1 C WATER   RESERVE LIQUID

                        UNSHELL CLAMS, CHOP, SET ASIDE

3 C POTATOES, DICED
2 ONIONS, DICED
6-8 SLICES DICED BACON, BROWNED, DRAINED   PLACE IN CROCKERY-POT
1/2 CUBE MARGARINE
1/4 C FLOUR, DISSOLVED IN COLD WATER   COOK AT LOW, 4-6 HOURS
2 C MILK
SALT, PEPPER   MIX CHOPPED CLAMS
1 TSP WORCESTERSHIRE SAUCE   INTO CROCKERY-POT
CLAM LIQUID FROM STEAMING CLAMS   JUST BEFORE SERVING

70

```
2 C  LENTILS, SOAKED OVERNIGHT, DRAINED          PLACE IN
3 SLICES BACON, DICED                            CROCKERY-POT
1 ONION, CHOPPED
2 CARROTS, GRATED                                COOK AT LOW,
2 STALKS CELERY, DICED                           ALL DAY
2 T  DRIED PARSLEY
1 TSP  GARLIC JUICE
SALT, PEPPER
1/2 TSP  OREGANO
2 T  VINEGAR
1 (16-OUNCE) CAN STEWED TOMATOES
WATER TO FILL CROCKERY-POT, 1/2-INCH FROM TOP
```

SOUP/MENUDO

```
NOTE:  TRIPE DOES NOT APPEAL TO
       EVERYONE, BE CAUTIOUS IF SERVING GUESTS

4 LBS CRACKED VEAL KNUCKLES, OR BEEF SHINS       PLACE IN
3 LBS TRIPE, IN PIECES                           CROCKERY-POT
4 CLOVES GARLIC, MASHED
2-3 ONIONS, MINCED                               COOK AT LOW,
1 TSP  SALT                                      ALL DAY
2 TSP  OREGANO
1 T  CHILI POWDER
1 TSP  CORIANDER
WATER TO FILL CROCKERY-POT, 1/2-INCH FROM TOP

1 (16-OUNCE) CANS  HOMINY, DRAINED    ADD, COOK 30 MINUTES TO
                                      HEAT AND BLEND FLAVORS

CILANTRO, FINELY CHOPPED
GREEN ONION TOPS, CHOPPED             GARNISH SOUP TO SERVE
```

71

SOUP/MINESTRONE

1/3 LB PROSCIUTTO HAM, CUT INTO STRIPS	
1/4 LB PORK RIND, PARBOILED TO SOFTEN	PLACE IN CROCKERY-POT
FAT, SCRAPED, CUT INTO STRIPS	
1/4 LB BEET GREENS, CHOPPED	COOK AT LOW, ALL DAY
1/4 LB SPINACH, CHOPPED	
1 ONION, MINCED	
1 CARROT, GRATED	
1 STALK CELERY, DICED	
1 CLOVE GARLIC, MASHED	
1 LEEK, THINLY SLICED	
2 TOMATOES, DICED	
1 C CABBAGE, SHREDDED	
1 POTATO, DICED	
2 TSP SALT	
1/2 TSP PEPPER	
1 TSP THYME	
1 TSP MARJORAM	
1 T, OR MORE, DRIED BASIL	
1 TSP OREGANO	
1 T DRIED PARSLEY	
8 C WATER, OR LESS, DO NOT FILL OVER	
1/2-INCH FROM TOP OF POT	
1/2 LB PASTA: VERMICELLI, LINGUINI,	
OR TRENETTE	ADD TO CROCKERY-POT
2 ZUCCHINI, DICED	
1 TOMATO, DICED	COOK 30 MINUTES, OR
1 CLOVE GARLIC, MASHED	MORE, UNTIL PASTA
1/4 C PARMESAN CHEESE	COOKED, BUT STILL
BASIL, TO TASTE	FIRM - DO NOT
	OVERCOOK UNTIL MUSHY

SOUP/ONION

4-5 ONIONS, SLICED	SAUTE OVER LOW	
1/2 CUBE BUTTER	HEAT UNTIL	PLACE IN CROCKERY-POT
3 T FLOUR	GOLDEN BROWN	
1 T SUGAR		COOK AT LOW, ALL DAY

3 CANS BEEF BROTH (BOULLION)	
1 CAN WATER	
WORCESTERSHIRE SAUCE	
SALT, PEPPER	

THIN SLICES FRENCH BREAD, TOASTED	SERVE SOUP IN BOWLS WITH
AND BUTTERED	TOAST FLOATING ON TOP,
MOZARELLA CHEESE (OR PROVOLONE)	COVERED WITH MOZARELLA,
SLICED PAPER-THIN	HEAVILY SPRINKLED
PARMESAN CHEESE	WITH PARMESAN AND BROILED
	UNTIL CHEESE MELTED

```
3 LBS  OXTAILS              DREDGE IN          PLACE IN CROCKERY-
FLOUR                       FLOUR, BROWN       POT
2 CLOVES GARLIC, MASHED     IN OIL
OIL                                            COOK AT LOW, ALL
                                               DAY
4 STRIPS DICED BACON, BROWNED, DRAINED
1 TSP  LEMON JUICE
1/2 C  CARROTS, GRATED
1/2 C  CELERY, DICED
1  ONION, DICED
1 C  POTATOES, DICED
2 TSP  SUGAR
SALT, PEPPER
1 T  WORCESTERSHIRE SAUCE
3  WHOLE CLOVES
3 C  TOMATO JUICE
2 C  WATER (OR LESS, FILL ONLY TO 1/2-INCH
             FROM TOP OF CROCKERY-POT)
```

```
1 C  DRIED SPLIT PEAS, SOAKED OVERNIGHT,     PLACE IN CROCKERY-
              DRAINED                        POT
1 LAMB SHANK, SPLIT BY BUTCHER
1/4 LB  DICED BACON, BROWNED, DRAINED        COOK AT LOW, ALL
1  CARROT, GRATED                            DAY
1  ONION, DICED
1  STALK CELERY, DICED
1  T  DRIED PARSLEY
1 TSP  SALT
PEPPER
1/8 TSP  THYME
1/2 BAY LEAF, CRUMBLED
2  C  MILK
2  C  WATER
```

SOUP/POTATO, LEEK

```
1   HEAD BOSTON LETTUCE, SHREDDED
3   LEEKS (WHITE PART) THINLY SLICED        PLACE IN CROCKERY-POT
3   POTATOES, THINLY SLICED
1 TSP  DRIED CHERVIL                         COOK AT LOW, ALL DAY
1/4 TSP  BASIL
1   VEGETABLE BOULLION CUBE
SALT, PEPPER
1/2 CUBE  BUTTER, OR MARGARINE
4 C WATER (OR LESS)
```

SOUP/TOMATO, CREAM

```
3 C  FRESH TOMATOES, QUARTERED
     OR  2 CANS STEWED TOMATOES          PLACE IN CROCKERY-POT;
1 TSP  SALT                              COOK AT LOW, ALL DAY
1 ONION, MINCED
1/2 BAY LEAF                             MASH THROUGH A SIEVE, RETURN
2   CLOVES                               TO CROCKERY-POT

1/2 CUBE BUTTER, OR MARGARINE
1/3 C FLOUR, DISSOLVED IN COLD WATER     MIX INTO CROCKERY-POT;
1 C  MILK                                TURN TO HIGH, AND COOK
1 C  CREAM                               UNTIL THICKENED
SALT, PEPPER
SUGAR
```

SOUP/VEGETABLE

```
1 CARROT, GRATED
1/2 TURNIP, GRATED                       PLACE IN CROCKERY-POT
1 STALK CELERY, DICED
1 POTATO, GRATED                         COOK AT LOW, ALL DAY
2 TOMATOES, DICED
1 ONION, MINCED
1 T, OR MORE, WORCESTERSHIRE SAUCE
1 T, OR MORE, SOY SAUCE
2 T  BACON GREASE, OR BUTTER
2 T  DRIED PARSLEY
1 TSP  SALT
1 TSP  GARLIC SALT
1/4 TSP  PEPPER
2 T  SUGAR
1/4 C FLOUR, DISSOLVED IN COLD WATER
1 CAN V-8 VEGETABLE JUICE
WATER
```

SQUASH/ACORN, STUFFED

3 ACORN SQUASH, CUT INTO HALVES AND		STACK IN
SEEDS REMOVED; PARBOILED 10 MINUTES		CROCKERY-POT
TO SOFTEN OUTER SKIN		ON A SMALL
3 UNPEELED APPLES, DICED		RACK
1 C CELERY, CHOPPED	MIX	
1/2 C WALNUTS, CHOPPED	AND	
1 CAN PINEAPPLE CHUNKS, DRAINED	STUFF	ADD WATER
1 CUBE MARGARINE, AT ROOM TEMPERATURE	SQUASH	
1/2 C BROWN SUGAR, FIRMLY PACKED	HALVES	COOK AT LOW,
1/2 TSP CINNAMON		ALL DAY
1/4 TSP SALT		

1/4 C   WATER

TAMALE PIE

2 LBS STEW MEAT, COARSELY CHOPPED	
2 ONIONS, CHOPPED	PUT IN
1 CAN TOMATO SAUCE	CROCKERY-POT
1 (2-1/4 OUNCE) CANS SLICED OLIVES, DRAINED	AND MIX
2 T CHILI POWDER	
1/2 TSP GARLIC SALT	
1/4 TSP PEPPER	

1 (12-OUNCE) CAN CORN, DRAINED	
1 C CORN MEAL MIX	MIX IN SAUCEPAN AND COOK
1 (7-OUNCE) CAN GREEN CHILI SALSA	10 MINUTES, STIRRING
1/2 TSP GARLIC SALT	CONSTANTLY; POUR OVER
PEPPER	MEAT MIXTURE IN CROCKERY-
2 C WATER	POT

COOK AT LOW, ALL DAY;
SERVE WITH AVOCADO SALAD
BELOW

1 RIPE AVOCADO, MASHED		
2 T SOUR CREAM	MIX FOR	
DASH HOT SAUCE	DRESSING	
1/4 ONION, MINCED		TOSS AND CHILL, GARNISH
GARLIC SALT		WITH CHOPPED GREEN ONION
		TOPS

LETTUCE
TOMATOES, SLICED

TURKEY/BREAST, STUFFED

1 WHOLE TURKEY BREAST; REMOVE BREASTBONE AND
    PARTIALLY SLICE EACH HALF INTO SEVERAL
    LAYERS WITH A VERY SHARP LONG KNIFE

SEAL EACH
STUFFED SIDE
TIGHTLY IN
FOIL

1 CUBE MARGARINE, MELTED
2 CHICKEN BOULLION CUBES
1/2 C BOILING WATER
1 (6-1/2 OUNCE) BAG CORNMEAL
        DRESSING MIX
1 ONION, MINCED
1/2 C CELERY, SLICED
1 T SOY SAUCE
2 T SHERRY
1 EGG
3/4 TSP GARLIC SALT
3/4 TSP SAGE

MIX, STUFF
BETWEEN
LAYERS OF
TURKEY BREAST

PLACE IN
CROCKERY-POT

COOK AT LOW,
ALL DAY

TURKEY/BROCCOLI

TURKEY PARTS
1 ONION, QUARTERED
1/4 C WHITE WINE

PLACE IN CROCKERY-POT; COOK AT LOW, ALL DAY

DRAIN, RESERVE LIQUID; COOL, REMOVE MEAT
FROM BONES AND CUT INTO CHUNKS

1 PKG FROZEN BROCCOLI, COOKED & DRAINED
2 C WIDE NOODLES, COOKED
1/2 ONION, MINCED
1 C SOUR CREAM
1 C AMERICAN CHEESE, GRATED
SALT, PEPPER
SLIVERED ALMONDS

MIX ALL INGREDIENTS
WITH COOKED TURKEY

HEAT IN OVEN IN GREASED
CASSEROLE, TOPPED WITH
ALMONDS

TURKEY/TETRAZZINI

3-4 C COOKED CHICKEN, OR TURKEY, CUBED
1/2 C WHITE WINE
2 C CHICKEN BROTH

PLACE IN CROCKERY-POT;
COOK AT LOW, SEVERAL HOURS

3/4 LB FRESH MUSHROOMS, SLICED
BUTTER
1/4 C FLOUR

SAUTE, STIR INTO CROCKERY-POT;
COOK 30 MINUTES TO THICKEN
BROTH IN CROCKERY-POT

1 C HALF-AND-HALF

ADD TO CROCKERY-POT

NOODLES, COOKED
PARMESAN CHEESE

PLACE NOODLES IN GREASED BAKING DISH, ADD
CHICKEN MIXTURE FROM CROCKERY-POT

TOP WITH PARMESAN CHEESE AND BROIL UNTIL
BROWNED

76

VEAL/BREAST, STUFFED

6 POUND BREAST OF VEAL, BONE CAREFULLY, TRIM ALL FAT 1 TSP SALT 1/4 TSP PEPPER 1 TSP THYME 2 T LEMON JUICE	SPRINKLE LAMB WITH SEASONINGS	ROLL-UP, AS YOU WOULD A JELLY- ROLL, TIE WITH COTTON TWINE
1 PKG FROZEN CHOPPED SPINACH, COOKED, WELL DRAINED 2 T DRIED PARSLEY 2 T ONION, MINCED	MIX AND SPREAD ON SEASONED VEAL	PLACE IN CROCKERY-POT COOK AT LOW, ALL DAY
1 POUND HAM, GROUND 1/4 C DRY STUFFING MIX 1/4 TSP SALT PEPPER 1 EGG	SPREAD OVER SPINACH LAYER	
1/4 C WHITE WINE		

VEAL/PAPRIKA

3 POUNDS VEAL, IN 2-INCH CUBES 2 CLOVES GARLIC, CRUSHED OIL	BROWN, DISCARD GARLIC, DRAIN	PLACE IN CROCKERY-POT
2 T SWEET PAPRIKA 1 TSP SALT PEPPER 1 TSP SUGAR 1 CLOVE GARLIC, CRUSHED 1/2 ONION, MINCED		COOK AT LOW, ALL DAY
1/2 LB FRESH MUSHROOMS, SLICED BUTTER	SAUTE, STIR INTO CROCKERY-POT	
1 C SOUR CREAM	ADD TO CROCKERY-POT	
WIDE NOODLES, COOKED TOASTED, SLIVERED ALMONDS POPPY SEEDS	SERVE OVER NOODLES, AND GARNISH WITH ALMONDS AND POPPY SEEDS	

VEAL/SHANKS

SPLIT VEAL SHANKS TO FIT CROCKERY-POT OLIVE OIL 1 CLOVE GARLIC, CRUSHED	BROWN, DRAIN	PLACE IN CROCKERY-POT
1 CARROT, CHOPPED 1 ONION, CHOPPED 1 STALK CELERY, CHOPPED 1/2 TSP SALT 1/2 TSP PEPPER 1/2 TSP OREGANO 1/2 TSP ROSEMARY 1/2 TSP THYME 1 CLOVE GARLIC, CRUSHED 3 T TOMATO PASTE 2 CHICKEN BOULLION CUBES 1/2 C WATER 1/2 C WINE		COOK AT LOW, ALL DAY SERVE OVER RICE OR SPAGHETTI
LEMON PEEL, GRATED WITH VEGETABLE PEELER MINCED PARSLEY, OR GREEN ONION TOPS	GARNISH	

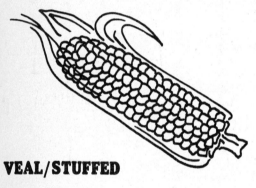

VEAL/STUFFED

3-4 POUNDS VEAL SHOULDER, OR ROAST, WITH DEEP POCKETS CUT FOR STUFFING		FLAVOR WILL BE IMPROVED IF TIED, STUFFED MEAT IS
2 APPLES, SLICED THINLY 1 ONION, CHOPPED 6 PITTED DRIED PRUNES, CHOPPED 6 DRIED APRICOTS, CHOPPED 1/4 C RAISINS SALT PEPPER	MIX, STUFF TIE MEAT WITH COTTON TWINE	BROWNED IN OIL BEFORE PLACING IN CROCKERY-POT COOK AT LOW, ALL DAY
1 T WORCESTERSHIRE SAUCE 1 CAN BEEF BROTH (BOULLION)		